HOMESTEAD
MEMORIES

by Linda Runyon

Homestead Memories

Linda Runyon
Wild Food Company
PO Box 83
Shiloh, NJ 08353-0083
lrunyon8@yahoo.com
www.OfTheField.com

ISBN 0-936699-20-5

All Art by Linda Runyon

Cover Art by Linda Runyon
Edit, Layout by Rosary Shepherd
Cover Design by Eric Conover

INTRODUCTION

Linda Runyon's active life has progressed through the familiar stages of child, teen, wife, mother, businesswoman, writer, teacher, grandmother.

However, her life has included some unusual (to say the least!) experiences that have led to additional designations unique only to her, which include: homesteader, environmentarian (one who eats from the environment), Weed Lady, and her most enduring title, Wild Food Woman.

In this book, Linda has recounted with aplomb and zest the difficulties and wild (literally!) happenings that taught her how to survive, and eventually flourish, in an often harsh and bewildering landscape.

This book is a collection of Linda's stories, photos, and her own delightful drawings, that depict her fascinating journey from a childhood enthusiasm for the great outdoors, to the status of internationally acknowledged expert in survival food skills.

Rosary Shepherd
Editor

CONTENTS

A CAMPER'S PRAYER

God of the Hills, grant me Thy strength
to go back to the cities without faltering.
Strength to do my daily tasks
without tiring and with enthusiasm.
Strength to help my neighbor,
who has no hills to remember.
God of the Lake, grant me Thy peace,
and Thy restfulness.
Peace to bring into the world of hurry and confusion,
restfulness to carry to the tired ones
whom I shall meet every day.
Content to do small things from littleness,
self control for the unexpected emergency,
and patience for the wearisome tasks,
with deep depths within my soul
to bear with me through crowded plans.
The brush of the night time where the pine trees
are dark against the sky,
the humbleness of the hills
who in their rightness know it now,
the laughter of the sunny days
to brighten the cheerless spots in a long winter.
Fill me with the breadth and depth and
height of "Thy Wilderness."
Thou has taught me by every thought
and word and deed.

From the early nineteenth century, reprinted from *Nirvana Lodge Log Book*, Indian Lake, New York.

THE EARLY YEARS

My great environment adventure began at 3 months of age. My parents ran a tourist camp at Nirvana Lodge on Indian Lake in upstate New York during the summers, and I stayed with them there until I was 11 years old.

Nirvana Lodge was a wonderful playground for me as a toddler and child, what with the interesting people that arrived every summer, the inviting lake, and the prospect of riding in a canoe! To the right is a picture of Nirvana Lodge in 1900. Note the cabin on the lakefront in that picture, which is where we stayed. Below is a clearer picture of it.

Nirvana Lodge year 1900. There were tents and lodging for 100 campers.

My intriguing summer adventures as a child were precursors to later similar episodes as a homesteader. Here I am wishing I were big enough to pump water from a well. I was six years old before I could actually accomplish it successfully.

And then there was the plague of the black flies every summer. Along with everyone else in the area, I suffered the persistent irritation of that band of relentless flying tormentors. Here I am covered in bites! Later, as homesteaders, my husband and I devised a successful method of dealing with those pesky insects.

The stack of wood piled alongside the wall of our cabin was my earliest indication that there might be some importance attached to building and maintaining a significant woodpile. Later on I would truly appreciate this introduction to that most basic preparedness action.

Here is a sketch I drew from my memories of my Indian Lake childhood days.

Following next are the first of my stories. (Remember the canoes at the lake?)

THE FIRST CANOE RIDE

The permission was given.   Rules applied though:

"Stay near the shore." "Go slow." "Don't go out too long."

"Take bug juice." "Don't forget your sweater."

"Thanks, Mom."

I followed them all, mostly . . . .

The wooden dock was still warm from the 80-degree day.   The creaks and water rippling out when I walked to the end evoked a fantastic feeling. *I am going for my first canoe ride, alone!* Throwing my bug juice and sweater in first, I had also brought along a flashlight. Maybe I might be out after dark.

I entered the canoe easily, carefully sat down, and began the slow paddle up and down the coast line of Indian Lake. I was watching out for rocks or sandbars and enjoying every minute. Insects began, bug juice went on, and the night chill began. On went the sweatshirt.

Time sort of got behind and night came in fast as I found myself all the way up the lakeshore, about two miles or so. I paddled pretty fast back towards the dock. It was pitch black when I approached, and that flashlight came in real handy.

Anxious to get on the dock, I got up and out too fast. The canoe tipped over, FAST, and I landed in four feet of water, FAST, and my parents were approaching! The boat floated off up the shoreline. I stood in four feet of H_2O while the flashlight stuck face up, shining so well up through the water.

"Did you have a good paddle?" they said. I will never forget my first canoe ride, as I watched my father go down the shore to rescue his canoe.

THOUGHTS ABOUT AN ADIRONDACK THUNDERSTORM

Being raised in New Jersey and used to those storms, the woods here seemed less threatening to me. "It will strike the tree first before me." I relaxed and actually enjoyed watching the storms over the lakes and mountains. The sound of them roaring down the lake deafened me, with displays of lightning that were just spectacular. I learned the hard way about being on the lake during a thunderstorm.

Now, it would be nothing short of sheer panic. When you are the ONLY object on the water, odds are cut down immensely. The first rumble I hear today sends me towards shore.

I was a merry teenager, paddling around rocks and islands, watching the ripples and not paying attention to the accumulating, threatening, storm clouds. I did not respect nature. The storm had rumbled many warnings and now it was here. Thirty mile an hour waves snuck up on my canoe. The waves began to tip the canoe from side to side, and my paddling soon became useless. I knew I was in severe trouble. I was dead center in the middle of a mile-wide lake.

My arms gave out fighting a hundred waves, and I sat waiting to be sloshed nearer one shore or the other. The blue-black boiling clouds sent down one lightning bolt into the water not one hundred yards from the bow of my canoe. A water spout shot up about forty feet into the air, sucking the water up with it in a tornado-like funnel. The funnel whirled some twenty yards near me and dissipated with a torrent of water.

I was mortally terrified. Throwing myself full-length in the gunnels of my canoe, I began to pray. The waves rocked the boat viciously and between the splashing and rain, the canoe began to fill up with water. Soon I was on my knees, lightning streaking all around, bailing with a small bait can from past fishing days.

Crack, hiss, OZONE smell, and I saw the air turn BLUE. How close am I to shore? Bail. Bail. Claps of thunder are beginning to drift to my left. The waves are lessening. I sat up in the seat again. I looked to the opposite shore to the camp I worked at. All lined up were several dozen tourists, cheering as I began to paddle my boat towards them.

The FINAL lesson was accomplished. In my embarrassment, I would always listen to the sounds of thunder and weather changes around me. I would respect Adirondack thunderstorms, always.

By the time I was 13, I worked for a camp owned by our family friends, the Gavetts. Due to my previous experiences as a camper, the Gavetts were happy to have me help them out during the busy summer months at Gavett's Camp.

The picture on the next page shows me with the other female staff. Duties included washing dishes for 100 people by hand, bed changing, setting and waiting tables, plus additional miscellaneous jobs.

At the time of this writing, the camp, now called Timberlock, hosts hundreds of campers during the vacation months.

Linda (front right) and staff at Gavett's Camp

MIAMI OVERNIGHT TRIP

The "Miami" is a dense Adirondack swamp next to Indian Lake; a twisty, turny labyrinth of tall reeds, grasses and moving swamp water. The grasses line the shallow, narrow maze. The swamp is literally teaming with life. Dragonflies zoom towards you as muskrat, otter and beaver dive by and below your canoe, while deer and very large birds stand waiting around almost every curve.

From trip to trip, the beavers provide excitement by damming up the way entirely, making portage VERY difficult in the swamp muck. Their woven sticks are a natural barricade to humans, while providing their families with food and shelter. We ALWAYS found a way around.

From start to finish, the Miami boasts a day or evening of travel to a natural island at the end. "The Island", as it is so reverently called, became the overnight spot, cooking spot, and restroom for weary travelers. On the island, the most fantastic meals were cooked!

In those days, wild greens were added to fried potatoes, soups, and stews, and the odors of our efforts wafted over the entire swamp, drawing an occasional black bear to watch our trek home.

One particular evening my parents and I and some campers began a two-canoe trip up the Miami. The lead canoe had the spotlight used for viewing animal friends, and I was fortunate to occupy the center, between the lead paddler and the rear. Sliding noiselessly "Indian style" we slipped past a blue heron, over two diving muskrats and by a gigantic trout heading downstream by the canoe.

Around a sharp curve and STOP! A gigantic buck was just lifting his head from the water. Water was dribbling loudly back into the swamp channel and our canoe struggled to stop quickly. TOO LATE we saw the broad side of the frightened mammal—I could have reached out and stroked his fur. The spotlight flashed up in the air, arcing frantically to keep him in its illumination, and leaving no room for his escape. We had unintentionally pinned him against the tall reeds.

Leaping like a steeplechase horse, and about that size, the 300 pound animal cleared MY head by a hair's length. The WIND from his shiny, sharp, bone heels all but parted my hair. CRASH, he hit the water over us with a smash, soaking all of us thoroughly and ploughed into the reeds all in one motion. We all could hear him charge through the swamp with renewed adrenaline for a mile or so.

This particular trip became the most exciting memory, and all others seemed tame from then on.

FACE TO WHISKER SNOUT

Evening was particularly black. Ebony black. I had come up from Plainfield, New Jersey the day before, to the mountains. Hot pavement, car paths, exhaust smells winding in the branches of the spruce, pine smell and lake water lapping at the shore line. An abrupt change from civilization to "freedom".

My job during the evenings consisted of Girl-Friday. On this night the Gavetts had just finished a delectable meal of brook trout. Of course, all the trout were hours fresh, and we all felt at one with nature on the outside as well as the inside!

"Please bury the bones in the backyard, Linda." The duty was plain. My mind tapped an order to me. "Go upstairs to your room and get your flashlight."

I loved the whole Gavett house. A big camp, holding maybe eleven rooms, giant old-fashioned kitchen, wood stove, complete wrap-around balconies, a breathtaking view of Indian Lake . . . even the old linoleum was a welcome change from city life. I fairly leaped up the narrow stairs to my assigned room and grabbed the flashlight off the old oak bureau.

I passed through the old kitchen, excused myself as the Gavetts were talking after dinner, and took the paper bag of trout bones gingerly in my right hand. Seeing an old trowel by the back porch, I picked it up and carefully closed the quaint screen door behind me. I took note of the small hole in the screening and mused at the amount of Adirondack black flies and mosquitoes that would pass through it before we got to fix it.

All of us were here to open the main camp: pitch tents, dig new cesspools, sweep, wash and clean, and carry dozens of army blankets and flannel sheets to summer homes.

Outside, I padded happily on the dirt. The smell of the pine and balsam was absolutely breathtaking. I could hear the Farrington Brook rushing rather quickly as I padded silently towards the mountain stream. Dropping the bag by my right foot, I knelt at a likely spot for a hole. First scraping, then seriously measuring the depth of the hole, I reached for the paper bag just as a deep throated growl reached my consciousness. All sounds of the lake, the brook and the wind evaporated and my ears focused on the distance of this growl from my face.

I brought my head up slowly and smelled the breath of a black bear exactly face to face. Bringing my left hand up with the flashlight, I focused the beam into his eyes and prayed simultaneously. Being on my knees was a distinct disadvantage to movement in any direction. My friend, as I addressed him in a tiny peaceful voice, was standing with his massive head and snout within two feet of my face. His paws were easily in position to whack me senseless.

In the three or four seconds of putting the beam on him and addressing him in my quiet voice, I realized he only wanted my fish. I brought my right hand up with the bag while holding the flashlight, which was a very stressful, insecure feeling. I had absolutely no leverage to whirl around and run, but addressing him by voice, I said plainly, "Here", dropping the bag on the ground just the other side of the hole, almost directly at his massive paws.

I dropped my hand, turned to the right by pivoting around on my knees, somehow got to my feet. I don't really remember anything after that until the screen door swung shut behind me. Breathless, I hollered to Bruce Gavett, "A bear, and he took the trout bones. Guess he was about three-hundred pounds or so by the head and paws. I hope he took the fish and ran!"

In seconds, the men went into action—bolted the doors, went upstairs on the roof, and showed spotlights down on the whole property. She or he bear was long gone. The garbage hole looked silly empty, but I for one waited until the daylight to fill it in.

Welcome to a summer in the Adirondack Mountains!

THE NIGHT I CAUGHT UP WITH BOBCAT

Many years have passed since I first saw a bobcat. It was in 1955 while I worked at Gavett's Camp. A spring-pole trap was waiting outside a garbage area for the cat that was raiding our kitchen area. My boss, Bruce Gavett, and the staff of girls including me were out on the back porch doing dishes for one hundred people, as usual. The night was as usual.

Clang, clang! The cowbell attached to the pole rang out with fury. We all elbowed each other to get there first. Running with dripping hands from the dish water, I went with Mr. Gavett as he wove his way ahead of us with a flashlight. The beam showed through the night, splitting the blackness with visual reality. A snarling explosion of fur was hanging by one leg.

The bobcat was smashing the air with clawed body arcs, spinning and hissing from his one leg, his eyes glowing red with fury. "Well, we've finally caught you," Bruce said calmly. "You have been raiding our kitchen for weeks now, leaving your floured prints up and down the counters." The bobcat had pawed and

13

explored every jar and box in the Gavett kitchen for weeks. Men sat up at night waiting for him, but he had evaded everyone until now.

As we watched the spinning, clawing, hissing cat, Bruce donned his leather glove and gently but quickly came up under the cat's chin with an uppercut. The cat hung in a pathetic, limp shadow. He was removed gently. Touching the ground, he awoke on impact, righted himself on all fours and streaked into the woods—a very lucky bobcat.

Knowing the Adirondacks as I know it now, most any other woodsman would have shot him on sight. We NEVER saw him again in the camp limits.

In 1956, the second time I met a camp fellow was as unique. The cat was following me down a deserted, wooded, dirt road. The road looped and curved and dipped with hundreds of potholes and log courderoy areas. The animal was following me abreast. I never heard him until CRACK, a twig snapped and I turned staring at a BOBCAT! The glint in his eyes told me his height was about the same as the spring-pole one. The game had begun. He dropped down behind me in the dirt road. I grabbed a stout stick with my left hand and felt better.

I climbed up on the grassy knoll on the left side.

The cat climbed up on the right side abreast of me. Be careful. This game of climb up, drop back continued for three miles. I soon began to see it WAS a cat game. When I rounded the curve back to camp, I walked slowly deliberately. He knew I was going to leave the game and he sat in the middle of the road behind me, eyes glinting playfully, lynx-like ears twitching. We stared at each other, and I stopped. Out loud, I thanked him for his company and the hour's game.

I often wondered if this cat was the same one that got caught in the spring-pole trap the year before.

My summers at Gavett's Camp came to an end and I went off to Monmouth Medical Center in Long Branch, New Jersey to become a nurse. This profession was of immeasurable value to me in my homesteading years. Here I am at graduation.

Shortly thereafter I married my first husband and had my three wonderful children: Eric, Kim and Todd. My great homesteading adventure began with my second marriage. I went with my new husband Ken and my son Todd to settle in a cabin on Lewey Lake, New York. Kim and Eric were raised in the city and were with us at the homestead in the summer months.

THE START OF MY FANTASTIC
HOMESTEAD ADVENTURES

Ken, Todd and I left New Jersey with an ax, sleeping bags, and great anticipation for the Adirondack winderness. Thus my homesteading experience, winter survival, wild foods, and just plain Adirnodack life, got underway.

Our first home was an unwinterized cabin on Lewey Lake. It would be our home for many years. We moved in at 20 below in the middle of winter, bobsledding the furniture down a moonlit icy path and over twelve-foot snowdrifts to our new home.

Here I am happily standing in front of it.

The winters in our Lewey Lake homestead taught me some valuable lessons about taking care of oneself in such incredible temperatures, and of course there are great stories to tell about that.

Additionally, the educational activities of my childhood years at Indian Lake, with the woodpiles, learning to pump water, and of course dealing with those darn black flies, helped to prepare me for the living conditions we experienced while homesteading.

MY FEELINGS AT TWENTY BELOW ZERO

I respect winter now because of a special series of events. The first incident occurred after I opened my eyes one morning. My head was stuck to the wall because my hair had frozen to the permafrost on the cabin wall interior. A layer of ice one-fourth inch thick covered the walls most of the time. My side of the bed was against the wall and I was unable to move. A haircut solved the problem. That was a not so typical twenty below zero morning.

I awoke another morning and felt a layer of frost on my upper lip and under my nose. I saw my breath as white as smoke and I knew the stove had gone out during the night. I slipped my slipper socks over the thermal underwear and went to the stove, stirred the coals, heaved in a few pieces of beech, and dove back under the covers. Listening to the crackling snap of the wood as the flames began was the audio security signal in my early morning. Outside the cabin, the air crackled with electricity and the next event was to begin preparing a fire, outside in the fire ring, for breakfast.

I settled on my haunches and turned the toast. In less than twenty minutes I was warmed on the front as I watched the ice crystals float by in the early morning sunlight.

I was relaxed in the crispness of the morning when . . . CRACK! A sound like an explosion came from behind me in the woods. I scanned the trees and saw that a maple tree had "exploded." The force of the explosion had ripped a big crack in the tree about three feet high.

As the wind stirred the frozen trees, they appeared to explode vertically. I often laid awake and listened to trees "explode" on a sub-zero night. It was a true wilderness barometer.

Another typical twenty below morning led me to

take a short walk up to the main highway, a mile up the hill. At the top, a friend was fixing her car. I thought, "How can she work with those immense mittens on?" I still had no real respect for winter. As I walked up to her, the big wrench she was working with broke in half. She looked calmly at the half remaining in her mitten and said, "This is the second one today." I was appalled and asked, "Isn't that a bit unusual?" She answered, "Not at twenty below." A wrench is really brittle when it is frozen solid and I definitely found my respect for winter enhanced. My friend cautioned me to breathe through a scarf when I walked long distances. "Your lungs will become irritated with the cold if you don't," she said.

Tapping trees at twenty below became a real challenge, with all the rules of survival used. More and more vivid memories added to my storehouse of education. The thought that flashed through my mind more than once a day showed my respect for winter. That thought was, "No wonder the Iroquois moved further south."

A tall outside chair after a typical overnight snowfall.

19

TWENTY BELOW ZERO PART II

As I began to learn more and more about winter, I decided to can my wild foods in the summer. I knew they would stay well in the seven and a half foot insulated refrigerator pit. I trusted my judgment enough for this experiment, as I had canned many times in my "city life."

Four hundred and twenty jars of campfire canned foods filled my storehouse. Winter descended and we were thrilled to eat clean jars of cattail inner pith, milkweed buds. Everything was delicious.

Then, the first of three weeks of twenty to forty below temperatures began. A blizzard snowed us in, but we had plenty of food. Winds howled, snow swirled, and when morning came, the refrigerator pit had to be dug out.

After the chore was done and the roof exposed, I opened the pit and climbed down the ladder with the lantern. My eyes blinked in disbelief. Every one of the four hundred and twenty jars had exploded in the intense cold. Stalactites and stalagmites of frozen food had oozed out of the broken jars and down the shelves into colorful ice piles at the bottom.

I was horrified and in complete panic. I got a shovel to scoop the jars off the shelves to search for ones that had just begun to freeze, and found a few jars that were just cracked or had pushed up lids.

Twenty below zero was an old enemy by now and this was a case of true survival. Canned and dried leaves, reconstituted and pulverized vegetables, and flour became our immediate food source. Even bark, ground to flour and used for teas, etc., became the normal procedure.

The refrigerator pit in warmer months.

ICICLES

Having a roof that was not insulated in the slightest, and a hot stove warming the cabin, the ice and snow melted at a great rate of speed. This gave us the largest icicles that I have ever seen under the eaves of our roof.

The average icicle was about four to six feet long, with a diameter of sometimes twelve inches or more. I could not lift them alone. My son, Todd, helped me with the chore of getting them inside. Placed in a bucket set into the top hole of the wood stove, the ice and snow would melt rapidly. One giant icicle might make four pails of water when melted. It was a true gift to the person washing clothes, dishes, wild foods, or themselves.

An icicle would often break on the floor and become a game for us. We squealed with delight as we chased the broken sections all around the linoleum floor of the camp kitchen. Sometimes, when I would send Ken down to get water, he would come back with one of those giant, four pail icicles instead. The sound of the ice hissing and sputtering as it melted was just the most comforting sound on a wintery, blustery day.

A ONCE A MONTH VISIT FROM THE OUTSIDE

The monthly visit from our landlords became the highlight of social interaction for my family and me. Lewey Lake, New York, held a particular isolated challenge for us. We as a family had no visitors, especially during the first long winter months.

City friends from New Jersey came up and spent precious time, but local people had not gotten to know the "strange" family in an unwinterized cabin on Lewey Lake. We often giggled about the logistics of people driving over four hundred miles to us for a visit with the town being eighteen miles away.

The winters were a real concern for me. I knew the problems of prolonged isolation and was so grateful when the snow machine whirred and I knew the landlords were coming on one of their welcomed checking runs. All our feelings ran very deep on the landlords' visits, and their questions were so thoughtful. "Do you need another ax handle. I'll teach you how to make one," Lynn said. "Do you have enough food? How do you feel? Come up to our lodge whenever you feel like it."

The snow mobile visits left me with necessary links to civilization and I went about my tasks with renewed anticipation towards another challenge of living within the outside. One with nature became the comfort and reward of those years at Lewey Lake. Thank you Lynn and Dorothy for the links to my own sanity.

FIREWOOD

Firewood becomes an Adirondack way of life. One has contact with firewood in his daily routines. Either bringing in the wood, or cutting the constant supply down, or up, becomes a basic routine. The woodpile is a security symbol attached to the average house and the feeling is unequaled when the pile is completed for winter. There is stacking of this piece of heat, the constant exercise, and adding to one's full sense of well-being.

Using only an axe, the time taken to fell a tree and cut it up becomes a day's work. The advent of the chain saw is next to the washing machine in my mind . . . a most necessary tool. (Many years went by before I owned a real washing machine.)

Ken cut all trees and firewood by hand for six years. I assisted. My job was to remove the upper branches and cut them up for kindling. They yielded hundreds of pounds of fine hardwood, maple, beech or yellow birch. These top branches became my way to relate with an axe. I could climb up on a downed tree, make my way to the tip and clear all of the branches from tip to bottom with a single sweep of the axe. Boy, did I enjoy that! It took me two to three years to perfect that skill, and I have since found that the accuracy of doing so never leaves one.

FIRE MAKING

I learned to become an expert fire maker through daily repetition. Kindling was gathered from around the area, and twigs found underneath the branches of a balsam or pine tree were used as tinder. Birch bark became my fire starter.

After a deep snowfall, the fire pit was dug out as a stove surface. Often, while preparing a meal, up to six inches of snow would accumulate on my head and shoulders. This condition would force me to make numerous trips from the fire to the shelter.

During spring and early summer we would cover ourselves with mud while cooking to protect ourselves from the many insects. Through torrential rains and high winds the birch bark always burned steadily.

Scanning the coals with my hand determined which areas of the fire would be used for each dish. To control the boiling of certain dishes, twigs of hardwood would be added to the fire. Constant tending of the fire and stirring of the food was necessary.

After a few years, we discovered sheet metal. I remember when the use of sheet metal became vital to the fire's existence. When I put the metal over a roaring fire during a rainstorm, the flames heated the surface to a cherry red color. This piece of metal became necessary for coordinating meals during these storms. If I threw the metal over a banked, hardwood fire in the pit, it lasted until morning. Sometimes when I was out on a food foraging trip too long, the coals saved were a Godsend.

My favorite type of rock ring was open on one end. I pushed the logs in as I needed them. Putting a new log on the fire meant fresh fire or flames in the surrounding area. I gauged areas for simmering or boiling by adding twigs or fresh logs. Hot rocks on the sides were used for toast or baking cakes, greasing the rock as you would a pan for best results.

Toast was fantastic when done over coals. I turned the bread when I saw the tiny coils of smoke appear at the edges of the bread. I learned to keep the bread to the edge of the fire to prevent burning the hair off my arms. In the dead of winter I enjoyed almost every minute of cooking over an open fire. There were times my back was thick with snow, but I was oblivious to any discomfort. Squatting in front of the fire and being responsible for my meal became a joy to me. If I were called, I might need a second call because I was intent on the fire and my work.

The personal challenge of foraging and cooking wild foods over a campfire gave me a special appreciation of my daily meals throughout my homesteading experience.

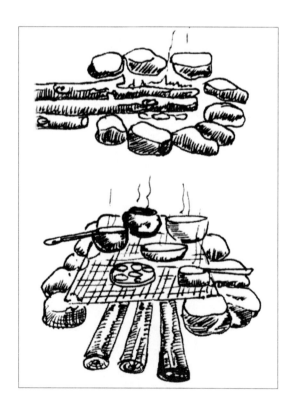

COFFEE CLUTCH

There aren't any adequate words to express the comfort, joy, energy, and secure feelings a cup of coffee gave me. Still does. Many memories flood back and hundreds of experiences make special cups of coffee remembered, even now.

The coffee break is more important than food, it sometimes seems. This break begins in an instant. "Want coffee?" "Yes, but give me a few moments."

Kindling, fire, water, and a treasured pot were gathered. Seems easy, but the skills varied according to the immediate environment of the day and of the season. Field or deep woods coffee, on ground or on snow, draught conditions, woods, swamps, rain or snowing, were just SOME of the conditions. Water from a moving stream was and is always best, but lake water was our source for years. Once the kindling caught the rest was easy and coffee was enjoyed!

This was our coffee clutch in the deep wilderness.

SPRING COMES TO THE ADIRONDACKS

The valley dirt was heating up as if it were in a greenhouse, while high mountain peaks held tight to their splashes of snow. As the white crystals melted away, the deep blue-black clouds loomed near the horizon.

To my left I could see spring gradually overcoming winter on the slopes of a distant mountain range. Spring melts removed the dirty snowdrifts quickly, displaying rotted branches and pine needles beneath the snow. Water from a newborn stream spewed from a rocky cliff. The face of the cliff caught the glint of a scarlet sunset, resulting in a light show of hot colors.

The beech leaves were losing the crinkly crispness of winter as the young beech buds pushed the leaves off the beech stems. Spring rain drenched the trunk of a large tree, stirring the sap and turning the trunk bark to an earthy red color. Grey rocks, devoid of snow, held red softwood needles in their crevices, matted comfortably in the warm spring sunlight.

The edges of the lowlands were covered with a peculiar yellow-green thaw water, puddled deep between the mud and the rocks. Egg-shaped mounds of moss began to grow over the dark, wet rocks. Much of the area was muddy, but billions of shoots began growing toward the sunlight. Life was stirring everywhere in a renewal of energy after the long winter.

WATER IN THE WILDERNESS

Water is a basic need for all of us, but when you live in the city, you take it for granted.

Our transition from city water to wilderness water was a monumental adjustment. Ken did most of the water hauling, but there were many days when I shared the burden, carrying the five-gallon container on my back. The feeling was one of extreme satisfaction—filling, hefting, and toting the container to camp to supply our water needs for several days. I would use the drinking water one day and then use the leftover water for cooking, washing, and preparing food.

Sometimes I feel that wilderness water is the sweetest, most satisfying water there can ever be.

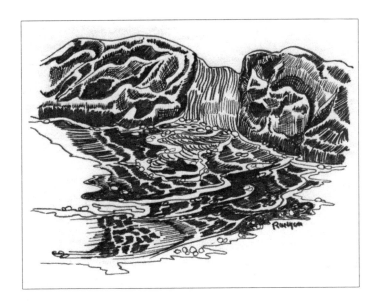

THE ADIRONDACK BLACK FLY

There are no words to explain this tiny, black-winged predator. When I bother to catch two black flies and bottle them up to send to my brother Paul in Arizona, you can believe there is a deep significance. Paul and I were raised in the Adirondacks during the summer and experienced the full impact of the black fly.

Until I received at least thirty bites a season, I was not immune. It seemed I needed this amount to tolerate the hot, swollen itch that resulted from the bites. The problem with the black fly is unique. Long after the initial bite has faded, one more bite anywhere on the body causes the previous ones to react again in the same way. At least one person a year is carried off the golf courses in the area because of a reaction to the black fly bites.

During my Gavett summers I helped pitch tents for Bruce Gavett. I held on to the center tent pole while Bruce worked with the heavy canvas, stretching it to fit. While he worked around me unrolling canvas, I remember a black cloud of flies coming toward us to get a treat. Hanging on to the center pole, I was unable to brush them off as they dove into my ears and eyes, and my bare arms became covered with more than 400 bites. After the tent was up I asked my boss for a bottle of 6-12 bug repellent. Covering myself with the liquid, I prepared for the next tent.

I soon found that black flies love to dive, swim, bite, and die in the 6-12. Immunity to the black flies was hard to come by and took several years to acquire.

Working outdoors with the black flies for twelve years gave me a complete understanding of why one uses bug repellent. I soon learned to cover myself with mud while outdoors, which is an old Iroquois Indian method. Sort of a natural ceramic shield, mud was the only method that worked, except heavy smudging. (Building a smudge pot is covered in *The Essential Wild Food Survival Guide*.)   I learned to make instant smudges wherever I was and to bathe my arms and hair in the smoke.

I taught myself to communicate with the black flies, and talked to them and disappeared from them mentally at will.   This particular skill improved throughout the years. The vibrating clouds of black flies around people are the norm for the Indian Lake area. A person can be seen standing on a street corner with a two- or three-foot cloud of insects virtually vibrating around them. Once in a while one will dart at the person and bite, but the mental state of the mind prevails.

Black flies teach us pure survival!

Smudge pot

HERE'S MUD IN YOUR EYE

Black flies biting even the corner of my eyes was the course of the day by 9:00 a.m. By noon the outside of my upper arms was filled with itching lumps, the back of my neck bleeding from my scratching, and I had swallowed at least four of the beasts.

Bottles of insect lotion were used. Even the spray kind bought from the new Grand Union in Indian Lake was not working. The problem was so great all of us were sick most of the time from the toxins in our body, both from flies and chemicals.

I can remember coming home to a prostrate husband once who was bloated and swollen from at least 400 black fly bites and sporting a temperature of over 103 degrees. Benedryl was the solution more than once for severity of black fly bites in the wilderness! Smudges kept the insects away and became a skill we excelled in. Smoke wafted from campfires, pails, old upside down wastepaper baskets, you name it!

Then I discovered mud! It dawned on me one day while getting water down at the stream. Why am I suffering so? Out of repellent, no time for a smudge, my hand scooped down and splattered mud on my upper arms. A quarter inch thick was smoothed on in a jiffy. "Let's see what happens," I thought. The flies zoomed in and out—foiled completely by the almost ceramic shield. Soon the sides of my face up to my eyes were thick in mud. I applied some to my nose center, bridge and tip, ear lobes, back of my neck and back of each hand.

Sitting still without fear, I watched the flies, zooming around, zooming in on smell, out and away at the same time. It works! Why didn't I think of this before? Walking home, it never dawned on me how I looked. When the boys saw me, they said the expected, "What in the world are you doing?" I remember saying, "Get used to it!" And they did, and I did, and here's mud in your eye, literally! But no more insect repellent for me! Facials are a part of my life every day, even today.

CHANGING FROM THE
MONETARY SYSTEM

The process of living free is not an overnight process. In fact, the whole mental change came very, very slowly with a gradual adaptation—NECESSITY RULES!!

Do it yourself. If you cannot make it yourself, adapt. If you cannot find the food you need, adapt. If you cannot find shelter, make it. If you are cold, make a fire. If you cannot take a bath, live with yourself until you can!!

All these changes brought about the change necessary to adapt to a free lifestyle. But free in the lack of monetary needs, not free from the constant 1) building, 2) splitting wood, and 3) food seeking. These three things made up a twenty-four hour period with only hours in between to actually enjoy the lifestyle.

As with anything else, you needed to enjoy each project. I loved projects. They fulfilled my day. I always set a goal:

> Move two cords of wood,
> Trim that maple Ken cut down,
> Re-screen the windows the coon came in,
> Drive nails backwards in the door against a bear
> attack,
> Bathe the mule and dogs,
> Clean out the stalls,
> Milk the goats,

Gather food,
Sterilize jars for canning,
Roll a log storage unit into place and sheet
  metal it,
Build a teepee storage unit,
Reinforce the outhouse,
Clean the camp,
Build the shelves into Todd's room,
Build a rabbit hutch,
Skin a rabbit for tanning,
Cut and salt the meat for dinner,
Pick enough daisy heads for two gallons of
  wine,
Pick raspberries for dinner,
Make jelly,
Hunt a quail for stuffed dinner,
Take the boat and cut enough cattails for a good
  supply,
Rebuild the wash area in the stream,
Roll rocks and reinforce the rinse area,
Gather moss for the black fly smudges,
Gather and wash a winter's supply of milkweed
  for pickling,
Cut and store enough kindling for canning two
  hours over the campfire,
Can one dozen cattail or milkweed pickles,
Take the saw and cut cattail roots, break fibers,
  and dry for flour,
Travel the stream north until I find a supply of
  mint, come back south and add to this supply,
Make Epsom salt and Vaseline poultices for
  application on mule's fly-infested legs,
Take mule in pickup truck to vet,
Hunt frogs' legs at night,
Make food wreaths and crafts at night,
Brush dogs and replenish dog houses,
Clean up and replenish chicken house,

Gather moss and chink logs of outhouse and
  storage areas,
Peel birch bark for fire starters,
Dig worms then fish for dinner,
Wash clothes,
Break up icicles for wash water in winter,
Snowshoe to a supply of cattail fluff for stuffing
 (milkweed fluff and poplar fluff in spring),
Make quilts from dump scrap clothing,
Make curtains from scrap clothing,
Build and maintain fire for three months,
Etc., etc., etc.

The day was planned and the job finished when
the goals were reached. In between, I felt "on vacation"
while gathering food, salads, soups, etc., for lunches.
And, tired as I was, I enjoyed every minute of getting
dinner and hearing my family's chit-chat from the
day. Bedtime was usually by 9:00 p.m. every day, but
sometimes 8:00 p.m. was necessary.

Lewey Lake

THE HOMESTEAD AT
LAKE ABANAKEE

We moved from Lewey Lake to the old McConnel place on Lake Abanakee. This house was too big to heat, so in the colder months the entire left side was blocked off by heavy rugs obtained in the dump. I for one am proud of our ingenuity!

Additionally, this farmstead was isolated from town so Todd had to walk 2 1/2 miles just to get to the schoolbus pickup site. One of the pluses of Todd's long walk was that he made many new friends, such as the fawn that toddled out to him for petting. There were a number of other animals friends that we met at this place.

STARTING THE OLD
CHEVY TRUCK

There were many old trucks. Usually there was no problem getting them started, but those bitter Adirondack winters presented some formidable challenges.

Here is the set of rules we devised for those circumstances:

Rule #1. Don't even think of starting the truck until noon.

Rule #2. To get an approximate temperature check, put your head out the door, breathe white smoke, and inhale using your nose. After two or three inhales, ten or twenty below zero will be apparant as your nostrils stick together when pinched. That is how we judged the temperature, and anything above that was a Godsend!

Rule #3. Gather a metal pail load of hot coals from the stove and run them under the motor area. This helps to get the kinks out!

Rule #4. Climb in the frozen seat and try the ignition. If the sun has shown on the hood long enough, the chances of getting the truck started now double as the coals give way to the last of their risen heat.

Chug, whirr, chrrug, cheroroom . . . the old Chevy turns over at a grinding twenty below zero. From the exhaust, plumes and plumes of white steam billow up as the engine runs more smoothly.

One silently gives thanks repeatedly as you pull the heater button over.

Such is a common winter's day miracle to the Adirondacker!

THE MANY FRIENDS ON THE PATH

Trekking to the water hole became a daily adventure. Both furry and reptilian friends as well as, it seemed, the entire insect world, seemed to present themselves from grasses, woods, or water, most often during warmer months.

We all enjoyed the daily sights and counted the appearances carefully. Dinner talks logged who, when and where, and for how long. Pudgy, a very pregnant garter snake, came out often. She never was aggressive, appearing slowly, slithering across the path. We all loved Pudgy, especially Todd.

Winder, a very crippled rabbit, jumped out and stared with his usual wide-eyed look. He appeared in my path so often I remember telling him out loud to "knock it off." I always had to stop and wait until he crookedly hopped off, for fear he'd have a "rabbit heart attack!"

Of course, any number of chipmunks, raccoons, and the occasional fox became the usual. The larger "pets" included deer and black bears.

Raccoons were large, fat, or skinny, small, all cute, but potentially dangerous. Raccoons were smiling one minute and hissing-scrappy the next. We fed probably dozens over the years, but never handled them. Once an entire band came through open summer windows and destroyed my kitchen. They even worked the Bufferin bottle open, emptying the contents. Marauders!

Frogs, lizards, salamanders, and small garters always popped into view. I couldn't count the hundreds of field mice and chipmunks chirping away, darting here and there.

Larger friends always were a dinner conversation. "Hey Mom, I almost caught a bobcat today," or, "Boy, that bear that walked by really smelled." "How close?" I would shout and Todd would answer, "I could have touched him easily."

We stayed far away from "bee" hunters!

The water hole path was traveled at night often. I was able to run easily touching the sides of bushes, trees, as a navigation tool. But, even with my "awareness at night", I still ran, woomph, into a smelly four hundred pound bear, just like a bear rug. I excused myself out loud, backed up and retreated quickly. I can only remember stepping on one paw!

HOUSEHOLD PETS

The last fourteen years were full with many pets. Pets of all sizes, shapes, and descriptions. The most vivid are as follows:

Herman, the garter snake,
Devil, the weasel,

40

Crackers, the white mouse from New Jersey,
Hoppity, the wart toad,
Winder, the crippled rabbit,
Pudgy, the pregnant garter snake,
Rocky, the raccoon, and his family of fifteen,
Bufferin Kid, the chipmunk,
Big Red, the chicken,
Banty, the banty hen, plus at least forty
  children,
Many dogs and their litters,
Bobcat,
Several deer, bear, goats and their kids (I
  delivered three),
Cats, Kiwi especially, and Claude, our neutered
  tom,
Fred, the guinea pig from New Jersey,
Barton, my dwarf bunny (I kept him until our
  next move)

Herman was a medium-size garter snake. He loved to sleep on a shelf in the living room, coming and going from who knows where.   Untouched by brooms, or harm's way, he became a part of Todd's life.   The shout came one glorious morning.   "I touched him!"   Herman stayed as a welcome pet until he hibernated the first winter.

Devil, the weasel, was a real problem to me. Popping up when you least expected him, red eyes flashing in the moonlight, or just catching him sneaking off the table in the firelight. He loved to appear behind me, Todd yelling, "The weasel is behind you." He stood coiled, hump-backed, and whirling, I chased him with my broom. He disappeared in a millisecond. I gained on him one day running round and round the back field. Devil seemed to thoroughly enjoy my chase. He returned to plague me several times and Todd seemed to see him first every time! When Devil was around, I was relaxed only when Todd was in the room.

Crackers, the white mouse, was smuggled across state lines in Todd's shirt on a Trailways bus all the way from Kim's house in Manasquan, New Jersey. My daughter, who is an animal person, bestowed Todd with Crackers for the 340 mile trip.

We all loved fat Crackers and let him slosh over the supper table, with his obese, waddly body after a wild foods meal. Extra precautions were taken with his cage, and it hung from a four-foot long wire, with a sheet metal sharp ring protector over the top of the cage. One morning brought the inevitable—Devil had struck. An empty cage greeted Todd one morning and I awoke to wails and tears. That weasel had slid down the wire, around the metal protector, somehow, and lifted the door of the cage. The next chase after Devil became the last. Todd ran in front of me around the field and Devil NEVER came back. We were proud of ourselves, but the depression of losing Crackers spread all the way to Manasquan.

Todd went through a stage of bringing home wart toads. Why can't he like smooth toads? They looked like science fiction subjects. The special one, Hoppity, found himself on my breakfast table too often. I actually picked his warty self up once, instead of the spoon that was near him. Should I try to put this feeling on paper? I think not. Hoppity won a few jumping contests and certainly held his own when mauled by the dog, and accidentally stepped upon. He was a hardy, warty soul.

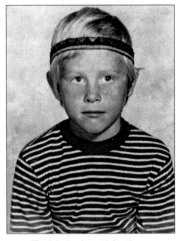

Todd during this time, at age 6.

Winder was our favorite black crippled rabbit and he had spunk! He had been accidentally stepped upon when young and lived to tell about it. He was truly a pet to remember. His leg healed, but he always went sideways from then on. He would wind his way through the grass, sideways. He "grinned and beared" his back and leg defect and lived to be the oldest and most popular rabbit to watch for. A true survivor!

Pudgy was a legend of her kind. Kim and Eric screamed, "Come quick, Mom!" A giant snake, "Humongous," they shouted. She was! Pudge was a four-foot garter snake, pregnant with hundreds of babies, looking like a small Anaconda that had swallowed a rabbit. The children, Eric, Kim and Todd, followed her alongside. She was seen several times again, and one day appeared her slim self. All the tiny garters scampered here and there for several weeks, and the children actually tired of catching Pudgy's children. They certainly became friendly to the people in the area. One had to watch his step at all times. Dozens of her likenesses grew to maturity around our camp. Many rescues were performed when the dog met one of Pudgy's children.

The Bufferin Kid, a special chipmunk, entered the room with a haughty squeak, characteristic tail twitching and climbed high on my kitchen shelf. He placed his paws around the cap of the Bufferin bottle and pushed and strained in front of our eyes. Pop, the lid snapped off. Reaching inside with a tiny paw, this chipmunk popped a Bufferin in his mouth and with cheek bulging, scooted down and out of the kitchen. No one could believe his eyes! No one else believed me either. The drug heist was witnessed twice by our family, until I removed the bottle. This Bufferin Kid was not unlike many of his cousins.

I waged a silent war with chipmunks for almost twelve years. Their cuteness when tiny feet squeaked across the shiny surface of the kitchen table, dropped into your pocket after a peanut, and squeaked back across, became a norm for after-dinner entertainment. But, these cute fellows sneaked almost everything I owned that was small enough to fit in their cheeks. Pennies, nuts, seeds, leftovers, medicines, shiny objects, all began to go the same route.

Goats became favorites of all of us. They were so cute. Our Mama presented us with twins after she met a neighbor's ram. Before Mama and her children went back to live with their former owners, we enjoyed goat's milk every day and made cheese. Hauling a goat to the vet nearest to Indian Lake was an eighty mile round trip in the back of the pickup. A trip any farmer can do without.

Our chicken, Big Red, was thirteen years old when she died. Impossible, but TRUE. Mr. Burgess, an old friend, gave her to me when Red was four years old. She had withstood a vicious winter and innumerable predators. Red ran free in the woods with Banty. Banty Hen, a small beach hen, presented over forty children to the family. We never ate the chickens as they were a source of enjoyment and eggs. Many children visited my home and carried Big Red around with them. She was the biggest, most docile hen. I miss her.

I brought Barton, the dwarf Rabbit, from New Jersey. My daughter and I picked him out for my oldest son's magic hat trick. He was too big for the act, and so he was a companion for a long time. Barton was definitely the last of the Mohicans, of the rabbit type, in the pet realm for me.

RAISING RABBITS

Raising rabbits for good came after the hunting began. Seeking plants and other chores became time consuming and it seemed logical to hunt and trap for food. Whether it be wood gathering, fire building, food gathering, preparation and cooking, feeding three was the daily goal. I hunted with a .22 rifle. A .22 was the only weapon I ever had. I was adept at bringing home grouse, woodcock, and an occasional rabbit. Raising rabbits seemed to be a logical turn of events.

One pair led to eighty rabbits within five months. I began to think of fall. Canning rabbit meat was suggested by an expert canner. I had tasted venison, but I could not bring myself to shoot a deer after following their lives so closely. I could can rabbit for storage. Wild food foraging was 60%, meat and fowl 20%, goat's milk and eggs 20% at this point.

I threw rocks at one end of a lumber pile and scoped the rifle carefully. I would heave a rock, scope the cross-hairs and, lo and behold, he would hop out, ears twitching with a wary look in his eyes. "Wham", he rolled over, righted himself and ran sideways. "Wham", I always hit my target. I would go over, jubilant, and pick him up by the hind legs, carry him to the stump, skin him out, and salt water him overnight. Sometimes he was still warm when he reached the chopping block.

It is very hard to write this story, but I repeated this "survival" act many times. My family enjoyed rabbit stew and remarked on how good it was many times.

THE ICE CREAM SAGA

We were overwhelmed when a truck from Grand Union pulled into the dump. Ken and I were doing our thing looking for new kitchen dishes. They never matched, but I gloried in a whole tossed out dish, or glass, or cup. A cheap replacement for our cabin.

Here comes the truck. I couldn't believe the dozens and dozens of boxes being tossed into the dump. Outdated half-gallons of ice cream! Many, many years had gone by since either of us have even tasted it!

It didn't take long to fashion a spoon from the clean, cardboard tops. After the truck left, we dug in, Need I say, WE WERE IN ICE CREAM HEAVEN!

All 14 flavors were tested and I have laughed about this day for many years! Thank you for the continuing blessings!

AN EXCELLENT HOMESTEAD

The family moved from the Old McConnel place to the back of Dick Frulla's saw mill yard on Cedar River Road. Ken was now the trimmer/saw man for the saw mill. An old $100 trailer, just 20 feet long, was the beginning of a homestead to be used for several years. We added a second story on top for Todd to have his own room.

Note the "teepee" shape to the right. . . .

THE TEEPEE OUTHOUSE

The transition from the modern, automated world to the "do-it-yourself" world became easier and easier as time went by. As we adapted quickly to the daily challenges that faced us, building a two-seater outhouse seemed to be an easy task. Ken dug the pit and the rest was my job.

I began by gathering three long, cured poles from the woods and removing the tiny branches with an axe. I jumped on each pole to test its strength. Then I tied them together and tried to hoist them (unsuccessfully) into place.

After the three poles crashed down four times, I realized I should have used a live tree as one pole. I finally gave in and walked to the mill to get help. In no time at all, two people had the gigantic tripod up and over the pit.

Gathering poles is a science. First, you go into the woods and gather deadwood or leaning trees. Although they are light to handle and are fairly straight, deadwood poles are a hazard in the woods surrounding a home. Next, push the dead trees over and trim the branches off flush. This is called nibbing. Pile them in one direction with six or seven to a pile, putting the heavy end of the wood near the path. When you are ready to drag the poles out, start at the farthest point and return along the path the same way you came in.

The finished teepee was made of layers of these poles built thickly on top of each other. On top of the poles, slabbing from the mill finished the structure to protect it against ice, snow, rain, and time. Slabbing is the first cut from a log. It is rounded on one side, flat on the other, making it perfect for the outhouse.

For six years the outhouse served the family and, after being redone inside several times, it became the relic structure everyone visited in the following years.

These pictures show two types of outhouse structures used: the teepee outhouse and the log outhouse. The log outhouse is chinked with moss which is indestructible, grows in the cracks, and changes to fit the wood.

See me peeking out of the flap.

Log outhouse built several years later.

THE MORNING THE RACCOON SAT ON MY HEAD

Temperatures were in the twenties. The teepee outhouse was particularly frigid and frosty. The opening did have a warmer sunlight streaming through. From the center pole that ran down directly behind the outhouse seat, there was a muffled sound before my panic set in.

The raccoon landed on my head with a little sound. His small padded hand slid over my left closed eye and his other hand gingerly held on over my right eyebrow. I prayed.

I could barely feel his closed, sheathed claws, just the pads on his palms and five fingers. He was calm, scrambling a bit to step down on my right shoulder. I could feel his sharp nail or nails coming through my wool jacket. I prayed. Coming down so slowly, the raccoon climbed into my lap.

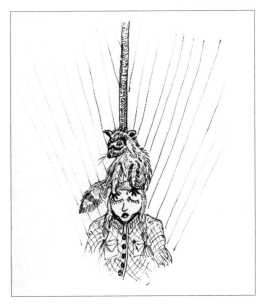

I did not move a muscle. I prayed. Down he went, so tame and friendly, to the frozen dirt floor and I could swear he looked back and smiled as my friend waddled out in clear view.

That was the morning a raccoon sat on my head. I will never forget that morning.

GATHERING MOSS

As the expression says, "A rolling stone gathers no moss," but the wandering homesteader with a paper bag and gloves will!

I would leave at dusk, heading for a new patch of woods. Mats and mats of moss grow heavily in most areas of the woods. I never ran out of areas to harvest.

Moss covers rocks, there are tree stumps covered in moss—green moss, blue moss, yellow moss, white moss—the types are many.

The green moss peels off the stumps and rocks easily. I peel, then roll the clumps, keeping the dirt side inside. Packed into the paper bag, moss clumps add up very quickly. A week's supply is gathered in fifteen minutes.

Moss is used for smudges (keeping insects away for hours) and numerous other uses. Pads also are used as chinking between logs of a new building, including our outhouse. I also would lay a sod-like peel onto a campfire for smudging at meal time to clear out black flies and mosquitoes.

The wandering homesteader gathered a lot of moss. By the next year the pads would grow back for another harvest.

Rolled clumps of moss

THE FORAGING TREKS HOME
FROM WORK

The eight and a half mile long Cedar River Road near our camp became a pathway to and from work at the Cedar River House. That historical building was known to more than one dignitary, including President Teddy Roosevelt. The motel at the Cedar River House needed housekeepers so for extra dollars, a truck, gas, etc., I went to work there for one challenging summer. Now no longer with us, the hotel is a memory I treasure. The trips to and from work are also treasured memories of my past.

Sometimes I asked for a ride, but sometimes I welcomed the long trek home. Words cannot describe the amounts of red clover (vegetable protein), crabapples (Vitamin C), yarrow (a potent stimulant), and dandelions (calcium) that were consumed on the trips. My endurance and energy were sustained.

The deer became used to my ways, and often I padded by without more than a faster twitch of their tails. Once, a bear that must have been five hundred pounds was standing by a tree near the road, eating crabapples. He raked the apples from the branches with ease, dropped down on all fours and pulled them up into his mouth. Crunch, crunch, the sounds were almost frightening.

I watched from a hundred yards, feeling very exposed and hearing sounds as if they were next to me. I waited more than twenty minutes for him to get his fill before I trod on. No need to disturb a feeding animal when one could help it, although I knew my own family was waiting for their dinner.

The walks in and out to work were very fulfilling, and a memory I am proud of in our homestead experience.

A typical handmade stove, no machinery was used to build it. A 55 gallon drum stove, nail and rock were the only tools. Banging away, Ken took hours to complete the folding door and repeated this for several stoves during the years.

PICKING RASPBERRIES
IN BEAR COUNTRY

The dirt road next to the shanty led down to an old log timber bridge. The bridge spanned the Cedar River that eventually dumps into the Hudson. There is nothing but private wilderness areas for dozens of miles. I crossed the river and climbed the wooded path for one mile. In another half mile I came to the largest raspberry patch I had ever seen—the same place my neighbors reported this story to me:

"A family and friends we know walked by our house for the second time this year to trout fish in the mountain stream. They came back within an hour. A bear had snorted and growled, stamped back and forth and grunted. Mother Bear had two cubs."

Would I meet them today? I padded on, with lightweight containers, a bucket, and fly repellent made from olive oil and pennyroyal. I whistled a tune as I approached the patch. I knew if I blended in too much the bears might resent it. This philosophy has worked before. I was allowed in their domain, or I was not.

I was aware of a very LARGE body leaving in the distance up ahead. I could hear and smell the bear shuffling slowly through the woods. I waited a respectful time and proceeded, whistling. Testing the wind for bear smell and listening with my ears, I whistled my way to the patch. The bear had left.

I picked with both hands, dumping into a clean, lightweight Chlorox bottle, and from that into the large bucket that I had placed in the path. I worked my way around the patch from left to right. Experience had told me I needed two hours of picking time for eight quarts of juicy raspberries.

I found many areas flattened by big furry bodies gorging in the juicy berries. A paradise for bear, deer, buck, any hungry animal. They wander in, lie down in the thick area, eat their fill, sleep, and move on. I picked eight quarts this particular day.

Thank you, Yona! (Bear, in Cherokee)

BLACK BEARS

Our family had a dog, one that delighted in nipping bears in the rear end as they ran off. The usual night descended, and a bear came in too close to the "under porch" of the cabin. Hearing the scuffle and hideous wild growl, I knew a bear was "in". The sounds of yipping and cay-ee told me the bear had injured the dog. I knew the bear was furious because the dog ran under the crawl space and continued to growl and growl.

Swiped, I thought. Now we do have trouble. No weapons, phone, or bear-proof door. Todd was safe in his room asleep. Ken climbed to the roof taking large cast iron pots with him and began the necessary din to keep the bear a distance from the cabin. I set the double bit axe by the front door and prayed.

I heard the bear crashing and growling around the house perimeters. First out back by the chicken coop, then on the woods side, and finally around on my right on the mill yard side.

Todd woke up and came in, rubbing his eyes and saying, "What's up?" Not too many explanations were necessary. The dog was still growling. Ken banged on the pots and the bear roared her protest.

At one point I heard her WAY down a hundred yards or more in the woods. I decided to make a fast break for the outhouse.

The attacks lasted for two days, on and off, until the chance came for a dash to the truck. The pictures show the bear trap the environmental people brought.

Being basically vegetarian, the bear never went in after the side of beef used as bait (would stewed apples have worked?), but did finally leave the premises.

Bear trap front view.

Bear trap side view.

THE DAY BUCK'S ANTLERS
BLOCKED OUT THE SUN

There I was, on my knees in the dirt in the jewelweed patch. Over my head, antlers moved in to completely blot out the sun. The buck moved silently, his patent-like leather hooves almost touching my bent knees.

To give the background for this story, every so often during my homestead days my family and I would yearn for a big "mess of jewelweed greens." Simmering in an open iron pot over our campfire, the greens have delicate green stems and leaves, which are a startling contrast to the bright orange flowers.

After simmering for 10 minutes or so we would ladle the greens into our wooden bowls and top them with butter, salt, pepper, spicy thyme and wild pepper seeds. Our patch of jewelweed in the woods was the biggest I had ever seen, or even imagined. I found evidence every spring that deer loved to give birth in the sweet, soft plants.

Another little-known but rewarding fact about jewelweed is that it's an effective antidote for poison ivy. What a funny feeling, to step into a jewelweed patch and pick, crush and rub the juice onto affected areas and have that irritating iching just go away. So natural.

That day in the dirt the weather was a steamy 80 degrees, and humid. In the woods it's a good idea to keep your legs covered, so I was wearing dungarees, and not the preferably cool shorts or bermudas. I was kneeling in the middle of a lush, dense patch of jewelweed and never heard a sound.

Then one small swish caused me to look *up* into a buck's knobby knees, and then *down* to the hooves, inches from my knees. The buck's antlers extended over my head and shaded the area. He snorted. I froze. A deer has razor-sharp hooves that support 500 pounds of weight, and that deer is in control of each hoof. I knew of bad accidents that involved deer hooves and people, and while accidental, those encounters could be gruesome.

Still in a frozen position, I prayed, "Please let this pass peacefully." With what seemed like an eternity, the buck flexed one knobby knee, snorted, and moved backwards very slowly. The sun began once again to stream into my eyes. The buck continued to move as if in slow motion and finally moved away. Snorting again he seemed to be saying, "Hurry up and leave my jewelweed patch!" While he moved backwards I had counted 12 points of antlers, so that buck was almost elk size. He was a "biggie."

After that experience I always proceeded my trips to that jewelweed patch with loud songs and whistles, to announce my presence. I heard several "lift ups" and shuffling sounds every time I approached the luscious vegetable and welcome medicine.

Truly a natural wonder—what a life!

ERIC IN THE WELL

Neighbors down Cedar River Road had a stone water well. Even the old bucket was intact, along with an old rope. My oldest son Eric was up for the summer and both he and the other children were cautioned more than once to stay away from the neighbors' well. The property was deserted, as the people only came up to their house in the summer.

Fall leaves were whirling and clicking down everywhere. One of the children ran down to our cabin shouting, "The bucket fell in the well, the bucket went in the well!"

Rounding up all the culprits was easy! While I explained again how the neighbors won't have water next year to drink, Eric said, "I'll go get it." For this feat, Eric ran and got many yards of "parachute cord" he had brought up for other uses, his sneakers, and a plan. Because he was only twelve or so I was close to panic when he harnessed up, got my husband to secure ropes above, and climbed foot by foot down into the freezing cold, damp chute. Hearing stones and pebbles fall as he went down lower was even more frightening. Way down in, he called up, "It's here. I got it."

Now the hardest part came. An extra rope had been lowered and the pail came up easily. Eric had the foot by foot climb up and out to do. The time stood still for all of us. I can remember Kim and her friend, and

Todd, Ken and I, silently peering over the wood sill of the old stone well. Only the sound of pebbles falling, falling, closer and closer as Eric appeared below us. Finally, he climbed out and we all cheered loudly. A magnificent retrieve by a brave boy. No one ever went near that well again.

THE AIRPLANE SURPRISE

Kim's birthday was coming soon. What present could a teenager enjoy here in the woods? My daughter had a friend up for the summer. Kim and Jill were enjoying the "free" life in the woods. I decided to give them both a surprise they would never forget.

The seaplane was hired for the special date. I was instructed to bring the girls to a runway of water used by a local seaplane pilot. His reputation was renowned and I had flown with him years ago. A scenic hour over the gorgeous mountains and lakes was planned.

"O.K. girls, we need to go get Kim's present," I said as we drove to the airport by the lake. "Why are we here?" the girls asked. "You'll see," I said. "Come on, get out and come over here to the yel- low seaplane.

Left to right: pilot's helper, Kim, Jill.

It is yours for one whole hour." The girls squealed, then screamed and then giggled all the way to the plane. This reaction was my memory for always.

63

THE OLD MINIATURE APPLES

The hunt for wild roses had extended to the sides of the main highway. The blacktop ribbon was a true link to civilization and the town on Indian Lake. The heat of an August day felt strange along the tar surface, and I realized I avoided the surface at all costs. In my mind the dirt was real, the highway was not.

The distinction between the two worlds was more than obvious. An obsession, some who knew me well would say. I never held back from saying this fact: "Here is the real, here is man-made, the not real." Come to think of it, I haven't changed at all on this subject, but thank God for the man-made, to teach people respect and love for the real.

The hunt was underway for the wild roses. Walking the ribbon of highway edge, I could see down hillsides and gullies easily. Every few yards I cut a right and headed to the woods. Gathering my thoughts, feeling a cool safety, I was ready to proceed another thirty to one hundred yards. I noticed that when a car went by I headed for the woods more quickly! Was I truly becoming a recluse?

No sign of roses yet. I found all sorts of acid run-off areas, stunted growth and over-mature plants at the bases of drain areas. I am always upset at these changes I see. Crash, flash of hide, hair and black hooves within "feeling" distance of my face.

The buck charged in front and away from me alongside a thick brush area next to the forest. His flag bobbed up and down, flagging his retreat along the asphalt. My thought was, "Stay down where it is 'real'". His great magnificent head tipped to the side and gave me a backwards look as if to say, "I know that better than you do!"

I climbed the embankment, always in awe of how neat it felt to climb facing straight forwards. I made a game out of walking forwards and edging sideways until I was up on the rise, walking on the sandy, pebbly shoulder of the road. This time I stayed on the shoulder and made time, walking fast for approximately one-half mile until I lost clarity and allowed my subconscious to take over.

All of a sudden, I dashed right and headed for the woods. There they were—gold and red little apples, hundreds and hundreds of tiny fruits hanging from hundreds of wild rose bushes. More rose hip than a herd of fifty deer could eat in an hour. I sat down and became "one" with them. Thank you, God, for leading me there again.

Each tiny apple being equal to an orange in vitamin C, I ate my fill, scrambling in a squatting position from bush to bush. Renewed, I was ready to pick a year's supply. Carefully leaving a bush here and there, I methodically moved from area to area stuffing first my pockets, then my scarf, then my jacket pockets. Running out of places, I went easily to a large burdock bush and gathered a few big "banana" large leaves. Filled with tiny gold and red apple-like rose hips, the burdock is easily wound up into a container.

After ten of these lightweight rolls, I began the long trip home. Thanking the area for my bounty, marking the spot for next year by the tall hemlock and gigantic pine paired together in seemingly guardian positions, I tucked my bundles up under each arm in even positions.

The walk seemed quick and the thrill of sharing the bounty with Todd and Ken was a perfect end to a perfect day.

BEAVERS

I was nestled in our home next to the saw mill, enjoying the stove heat on a crisp fall morning. I heard a crash echo across the back woods. I went instantly into a scanning a pattern and intensely listened for the sound waves. CRASH! The echo reached my ears. Beavers—must be!

I rushed from camp and thought myself as light as possible, treading over the forest floor silently towards the crash sound. I sensed bodies moving. Stock still, I craned my neck and focused on a wondrous sight. A beaver was gnawing, head sideways, in a crevice of a tree and had it almost chewed through. "Grey bark and white wood poplar," I thought, "and it is ready to fall."

Poplar is the beavers' favorite food, and I became aware of another beaver waddling with tail dragging to my right, away from the site. The beaver, chewing, raking his teeth down the crevice another time and "IT'S CRACKING", I screamed to myself, and he waddled backwards, reversed himself with flat tail dragging, and came towards me. A slight breeze caught the tree and it cracked twice and pitched slowly away from all three of us. It became my privilege to become part of their world, and I watched them chew the individual branches off one by one. The process took two days, and each branch was dragged down a mud slide to their dam for fitting in place and strengthening. The bark would be their food for a winter. (After spring thaw the branches would bob to the surface of the pond, stripped of their bark.)

That fall went into winter and then into spring. One day, the camp was exceptionally claustrophobic, but Todd and I persevered with his homework. We were working quietly when a horrible, almost explosive sound roared through the afternoon. I hollered to him and we bolted outside to the woods back of the camp.

My mind focused in with awful clarity. A wall of water with a 15-foot wave crested through the woods, exploding sticks in all directions like a porcupine. The wave roared towards us through the woods, and four PETRIFIED beavers body surfed in front of the wave, two adults, two babies.

The wall of water toppled trees like match sticks, and brush was curled up behind the crest, which was stretching out on the sides now, lapping closer and closer to my son and me. We looked at each other and thought the same thing—we would be OK. A grouse screamed and shot upwards, and the destruction grew closer and closer.

Todd and I looked back and forth and still agreed to stand our ground. The water played out in hundreds of smaller waves, grinding over the brush and leaves, floating trees, branches, beaver sticks, and then diminished a dozen feet from our camp. The pond behind the wave was gone, and the water swished back down to the small stream bed that led from the pond.

The next two hours were spent searching through the woods for animal survivors. Todd found mice, chipmunks, and two squirrels, but NO beavers. We figured they body surfed straight out to the river below. It wasn't long before they waddled back up and began to rebuild the dam from scratch. Our experiences attest to the saying, "Busy as beavers".

THE SAW MILL

My memories of the saw mill defy description! I felt like time stood still and the past memories of visiting saw mills with my father became the present. My father, Paul Runyon, was an expert furniture creator. He bought boards to make furniture for Nirvana Lodge. The same sounds beset my ears as when I was six years old. The whining, grinding, screeching and the awesome smells of raw wood being sliced became overpowering. Sheets of high speed sawdust shot from the gigantic log being peeled apart by the six foot saw blade. Peeled off just as slick as butter.

My home was at the saw mill for two years, and the sounds of this mill were a center of reality as I learned my skills in the woods with wild foods. I heard the saw about a mile and a half away and gauged my distance accordingly. Coming back from a long trek for food, the sound centered me.

In the mill, the edger man in red suspenders, with professional robotic movement, grabbed the slice of wood as it came off the log. He threw it with all his might towards the chipper slot conveyer belt. The slab continued into the saw blades of the giant chipper and with a whirr, became sawdust instantly.

The edger man turned, grunted and grasped an inch thick twenty-footer with brute strength. He sent it to Ken (the trimmer man), who stooped, grasped it in two carefully calculated places, and hefted the two-hundred-pound board up to the double saw blade. Zing, zing the trimmer saws rang out their high pitched sounds.

The board zoomed down the green chain to the green chain man, who also stooped, picked up the board and stacked it on the piles of thousands of pounds of raw pine, beech, maple, or white birch. All prayed on a fast day the saw would need repairing, so they could take a precious ten to twenty minute break for repair time. I added up the poundage one day and was astounded when I reached over ten thousand pounds per man.

I used to sink down a far wall in the sunshine, squatting on the foot-and-a-half boards of raw lumber floor. Thick pine walls with large gorgeous knots, grain, and a potent raw pine smell greeted me. I always felt VERY MUCH in the way in this man's world. I marveled at the freedom in which they moved about in a seemingly impossible task of lifting thousands of pounds a day without human deformity. I never consciously realized my world became the same relative to my individual potential.

I always got very hungry the moment I came in the mill. I felt much empathy for the men waiting for lunch. The smell of their peanut butter sandwiches was overpowering. One could feel their relief with the break, and while they ate I climbed down outside and foraged for my lunch in the nearby field. The men sat inside, or out on the deck, and chit-chatted. One might fall asleep when resting for five or ten minutes. These visits were special in my memories.

Watching the sawyer man overseeing the operation was the same feeling I got when watching a doctor operate. The immense responsibility of assessing the tree for the right size boards, setting the "dogs", lining up the logs with precision, rolling them into place, and other unknown qualities of a sawyer were his. The man smiled with pride as the boards peeled off at a speed he knew the men could handle in a day's time. Teamwork to the maximum.

Summer was much different from mud season. Winter's thaw is mud season. Trucks got bogged down, logs were caked with six inches of solid mud, machinery became clogged from the spatter of mud everywhere. Calm aloofness, grunting and turning in precision, the edger man continued without notice, and when he walked outside, he squooshed his way to the truck that might take an hour to haul with the dozer from the foot-thick mire. I squooshed my way to and from, also, and development of a large thigh muscle was inevitable.

Winter at the saw mill defied description again. This memory will always blend with the historic Adirondack pictures seen in museums. I am indeed privileged to have been part of what was true survival for all of us.

Men scaled icy logs, measuring the board feet for the day, pulling their bodies through the fresh snow, frost covering their faces and beards. Icicles hung from their chins; purple fingertips showed through the worn gloves as they hefted logs into place on the frozen chain. SCREETCH of the chain set the motion, and the whine of the saw followed. The WHIRR of the chipper followed. Then came the thud of the board as it landed at the bottom of the green chain.

Such was the pattern of sound of the Adirondack saw mill.

MAKING TWIG FURNITURE

During our days by the saw mill, Ken became quite skilled at building twig furniture that was sturdy, aesthetic, and very comfortable. I helped him in this satisfying endeavor by keeping the bins full of different lengths of wood, and doing any other furniture construction jobs that I could.

We had a sign outside the saw mill barn that said "Please Beep for Service!" We used the barn as a tourist storage area, and occasionally someone would come in across the mill yard and shop for a twig piece.

The old Hamilton town truck made many a trip to New York City filled with furniture.

THE ROADSIDE TWIG FURNITURE DISPLAYS

Those days were anticipatory. Would we sell a chair or a table? Maybe several people would stop, so make the display long and catchy!

Set up the smudges. The black flies will be horrible. Get a good piece of poplar to chisel away at a new bowl. Don't forget the wet towels and the fresh willow twigs for baskets. Load the truck. Make sandwiches. A wild salad will be fresh. Make tea ahead of time. Make coffee over the campfire. A selling day ahead! Often, the entire day would go by without anyone stopping. Some days, one or even three people might stop. The encouraging days, someone would buy two chairs, a table and order some special piece.

The furniture display days were so much fun. A part of civilization, a day to talk with someone. Interestingly enough, if one or more cars stopped we could hardly handle it. Our isolation had produced a one-on-one fairly comfortably, but more than one person talking at the same time produced a lot of stress.

These display days obviously prepared the "homesteaders" for the trips to New York City to come. Eventually, so many pieces of furniture were created that more than the Hamilton was needed for transportation and a van was rented. The rental van would be loaded and off the homesteaders would go to Manhattan, or Fifth Avenue, or even an occasional movie star's garden!!

DOWNTOWN IN NEW YORK CITY

I'm in New York City on business.

I walk the few blocks to a restaurant and enter. The streets along the way are busy and the graffiti on the walls is absolutely ingenious! I am appalled at the amount of people in groups standing around on the sidewalks. No words are spoken to me. I am aware of an undercurrent that is VERY NEGATIVE, ALMOST FRIGHTENING. My imagination is running away again. Outside the restaurant, teenagers play hard at basketball, led by one red-shirted expert, obviously their teacher. Moving in and out of the youths at precise times, he is doing a magnificent job of generating action and enthusiasm.

Ah-ha, I see deliberate joy in a musical rock movement, jive gyrations, my favorite expression of life, joy, body English, human freedom. An ambulance cuts through the happiness with a sheering scream at top speed, blurs by, a blur of white and blue. No one looks, or reacts visibly. But one elderly, pathetic man, limping by in what some may term "bag clothes," watches the blur and stands transfixed at its passage down the city street.

Inside the restaurant, the old shellac Life Magazine tables are a mellow color, having held virtually thousands of elbows attached to relaxed humans. The food is just fantastic! Aproned, cobra-tattooed teenagers weave with expert agility among the patrons and appear to me as top care givers in a disturbed environment.

From the restaurant window I see the park across the street clearly. This park is known to be home to many homeless people. Chaos meets my eyes as young ones begin their entrance for the night—tents on bushes, young mothers alone with tiny infants, old, sick, derelict people with their paper bags and one blanket, coat, or towel. While the basketball players have interested a group of young would-be's, the nightly parade begins, the homeless making ready while the black and dangerous night closes in.

Graffiti on the wall looms twenty feet in gorgeous colors—CRACK KILLS—and a pair of handcuffed hands is painted in surrealistic color, messages of truth by artists who care. The opposition is evident, the decisions are decisive. INSIDE, the people eat faster, as if knowing the darkness is closing in for that walk home. A child rubs his tummy and says, "I'm full," while the child outside clings to his mother's hand as she resigns herself to another night under a bush where the language is foul, the earth smells of urine, and children in the corner of the basketball court are now practicing karate. Dog leashes now appear in many hands walking by the park. From ropes, chains and leashes, as well as elaborate harnesses, the dogs vary in size but seem to get larger as the darkness ensues.

75

THE CITY AWAKES, INSIDE AND OUT AS THE NIGHT IS HERE IN THE BIG APPLE. Under the bushes, the world is now tuned out. Long, shiny brass rails seem to attack the marble floors as silent escalators move in unison running down into the cellars.

Graffiti is everywhere saying DRUGS KILL, SAY NO TO DRUGS. Skateboards lick over sidewalks at night, screams of protest are heard throughout the night, hushed private conversations are apparent as the rapid-fire discourses take one's attention. Screech of brakes always brings up my eyes and the laughter of children makes it all real. Glass bottles are thrown on a brick wall, venting immense frustrations. A sea of garbage meets the eyes and makes sidewalk footing precarious at times.

I enclose myself in a taxi. The taxi driver states (after hearing my story about a bear in our garbage dumps in the mountains), "I wouldn't like that! You would have to dress like Rambo to take out the garbage."

I love New York City! From my life in the woods the parallel is overwhelming, and I will always be grateful for both sides of life's fullness.

WINTER CAMPING

We are in the intense grip of winter's cold. The progression is a normal one for the Adirondacks. We adjust rather well from season to season.

Winter camping is simply a way of life for our family. Always try this close to home. Keep a safe place for a time, then go out further and further. Each snowfall or frigid night, windy gales will change the "routine" quickly. Winter camping should begin with a shelter, kindling, and campfire.

A nest of trees provides a windbreak, kindling for fire, and basic balsam food or pine tea. A grove of softwoods is ideal for any "long term" shelter. Kindling from under softwoods remains brittle and dry for a quick flame starter, or fast, hot flame for a precious cup of snow coffee.

When I camped in deep snow, I always used my bulk, feet, thighs, arms, to sweep snow aside, stamping an area down. A ten to twelve foot area will be the best. Then, using a tree stand as a backdrop, I visualized the safest fire area. Dragging several larger dead poles or trees to the ten foot area, I began to make a base of wood. Building up from the "raft base," a winter campfire will stay dry.

Think of your camping experience in hours. How much wood for one hour, two hours, etc. A few "dry" runs near a safety home will give you terrific experience. Another trick is hauling a piece of sheet metal for an instant oven and flat cooking surface, plus it will keep coals hot—sometimes overnight. Practice!

THE SNOWSTORM TO BEAT ALL

The storm descended quickly with swirling snow that covered the previous foot of snow like a veil. "Let's go into town and get some supplies. We might be snowed in this time," I said with some excitement, and the three of us headed into town to shop with the other last-minute shoppers. But it was already too late for us. Our home, eight and a half miles outside of town on a dirt road, had no neighbors, no phone, no electricity. "I might as well be in Alaska," was my favorite expression, but now I would truly believe it.

The drive back from town became a chore. It was almost impossible to see in the heavy, drifting snow, but the truck made the drive up the hills and was finally parked. But then I noticed a worried look on my son's face. He was gazing across the mill yard to our home a half mile away. The sled was loaded with the supplies, and Ken shouted to me to follow him. He would go ahead to start a fire. I was glad he decided to go first because those precious minutes to warm up the house would be vital.

The temperature had fallen to ten below zero, and with the wind chill, it was probably thirty to forty below zero. The wind had increased to blizzard force, and it became hard to stand or even move. Ken's tracks disappeared quickly as the snow came down harder. I made the mistake of calling for him and my son panicked. I tried to hurry, but Todd said he was scared. I told him to walk close behind me, and I plowed a deeper, more deliberate trail.

As we moved toward the center of the wide-open mill yard, I lost complete track of my direction. I hadn't the faintest idea where I was, but I knew if I came to the edge of any side of the yard, the trees would be there. This helped relieve my mind a bit, and I told Todd to sing with me. We sang "Onward Christian Soldiers, marching through the snow" as we moved toward what felt like a downward slope toward our home.

I shouted to Todd, "We're almost home." I had pulled his collar over his face and was almost dragging him behind me at this point. I didn't let go of him until we stumbled into the house. My glasses were completely iced over and clunked onto the wooden table.

We all found out what frostbite feels like that day. We laughed together around the stove as we realized what the natives meant by Adirondack blizzards. Three feet of snow fell that night as we enjoyed our camp by the stove. Adirondack winters were to be respected even more from then on.

In ten feet of snow a friend joins me in a winter coffee clutch.

THE DAY WE WERE SNOWED IN

I remember the day like yesterday! In the Adirondacks, the snow can drop a foot in an hour.

One particular night I know the drop had to be three to four feet on top of four feet already on the ground. When you have a total of eight to nine feet of snow you have a door snowed shut, windows covered completely, and a truck out of sight in a drift.

As usual that morning, I opened the front door. I thought the place was unusually dark, but didn't realize the snow had completely covered the window glass. The door DID NOT OPEN but a foot or so. Trying to push the door open was futile. How could we get out? No shovel, or any tool like a shovel, was in the house.

We ended up taking a dustpan with a handle, a big pot, and other odd things. Digging away a little at a time and putting the snow to the left seemed the best way. A tunnel was begun in an hour or so. All day long we worked at the dig. I never really got frightened until we were very tired and not seeing daylight in the tunnel.

When we finally broke upwards and saw the daylight, the sun had melted enough snow to form a crust on the top. About five feet of hard crust remained. It was so much fun to climb up on a box and climb out of the snow tunnel—we were free!—until we faced hours of real digging to free the truck, which had a snow shovel in it. We took most of the next day to get the truck uncovered enough to get that precious shovel out. I have NEVER viewed a snow shovel with so much joy! We did get another one and kept it in the cabin for future use.

It was a full week or so before a plow came in the mill yard and punched a route to the Cedar River. This was just another Adirondack snow storm.

One time enough snow fell overnight to bring

roofs and trees down. We soon learned how to attach two long hardwood handles, putting a crosspiece board on the end. It took a lot of strength, but you could swing the long tool in place and pull a lot of snow off the roof. My son became an expert with the roof tool!

A snow scene of our cabin (with 2 feet of snow on top), and log outhouse.

THE SNOW PLOW ICE JAM

An especially terrifying moment arrived when a blizzard hit suddenly. Todd was just getting on the bus to go down Cedar River Road. I tore out in the pickup truck to get him before the road was impassable. As I rounded the curve where the Cedar River flowed, an explosive boom sounded. The river, filled with gigantic ice cakes, rushed across the road and back again.

The scene ahead on the road was a shock, with ice cakes swimming in a foot or two of rushing river, just as the school bus came towards me. Shouting across, the driver said, "No way can I go over safely." Todd was terrified. There were two or three more children on that bus, all completely cut off from their parents and homes. The snow storm raged down and a couple of swirling inches had accumulated already.

The bus driver used a Citizen Band radio to put out a call for help. Nearby was the Indian Lake snow plow. They came immediately and called to me, "If I come across, you come back with us and ride the bus back."

As we were pulled through the rushing water by the big plow and using a stout chain, I felt fairly safe in the back of the one-half size school bus van. Creeping along, I saw a big ice cake approaching slowly, but past that I noticed the water coming in on the floor boards under the doors.

Todd screamed and pointed. Up on the seats the children climbed as we went up the road safely past the water. All the other children's parents were there also, and we thanked the men heartily. The plow pulled the van back over and we all scurried home as the winds howled and snow fell swirling.

This was another night I thanked God for our safety and brave friends.

THE FOURTH OF JULY IN DEEP WINTER

My oldest son Eric was visiting. This memory is crystal clear. Drifts of snow came up under the camp's windows. No one could drive in or out for weeks. Plowing through drifts was the most labor done these days. Chickens, mule, goats, and furniture took all the day's time in mid-winter.

Eric came in from the cold night and asked me a strange question, "Mom, did you see fireworks on Fourth of July?" "Of course not," was my quick answer. To leave the camp for town was a real major trip, and town had become more and more distant.

"Well," Eric stated, "you will see them now!" Darting outside again, the door slammed hard. What is he doing? Then all the outside lit up like the biggest fireworks show you have ever seen! Boom, boom, pop, pop, pop, the rockets great glare was on all sides of the cabin. Sparklers began to shimmer on top of the snowdrifts right outside each window. Cherry bombs boomed and rockets zipped skyward! This was absolutely amazing and I can remember laughing and crying with awe and gratefulness.

Fourth of July in December was the best! Thank you, thank you, E. I bet the deer, fox and rabbits were stunned for weeks! I know I still am!

83

THE THAWING OF THE UPPER HUDSON

The ice cakes have ridden up on rounded rocks and thinned from a few days of forty degrees. Slivers of huge ice wafers are cracking from the heat. Occasional hunks of ice slide by in the black, frigid waters, while the river channel opens up to spring. I am amused by the tiny birds, zipping and hopping among the ice, pecking sharply at newly sounded debris.

The driftwood level on the bank shows a high flood water from a few weeks ago. Layered like an ocean beach with wood and clam shells, the debris is formed as a result of a cleansing in the mighty Hudson River. An occasional tree slides silently through the center channel, bumping infrequently on a particularly thick ice cake still hanging on. The river moves with a dull roar, unlike the rapids down below. The sound is soothing to me as I walk on the banks of winter-matted plants.

Plants are old but greening up under the grass mats of winter's weight of snow. The whole area is as if washed by a giant hand of heavy water. Plantain is particularly green in thick whorls on the banks. The old milkweed pods still stand stately and askew, a monument to last summer. One senses the worms stirring in the softened ground. Certainly the awakening of the growth stage of nature's world begins.

From the thawing of the Upper Hudson to the greening of summer in the Adirondacks, a miracle within the time of nature is apparent again.

THE PRE-SPRING THAW

The Adirondacks had an interruption in the daily routine of snow flurries that had added to the two feet of snow on the ground. It was called the February thaw and it began with rain on the 22nd of the month. Within three days it was 60 degrees and there were bare spots on hills, around trees, and mounds of dirt appeared here and there.

Finding food everywhere under the snow is routine for me, but after a rain it is easy. The rain goes through the snow, loosening up the grass below and releasing the green from the permafrost of the earth's top layer—a perfect time to study the following phenomenon: When digging through the areas where leaves were mounded two feet thick, hundreds of plants are revealed growing prolifically, their tendrils a new chlorophyll-green, stretching between leaf layers and bound together with fine frost. Sorrel appeared to be the most common, a delicious vitamin C treat, with dandelions growing a close second, their roots exposed in some cases, and new roots having grown between leaf layers, white and succulent.

Under the hay layers I found hundreds of leggier sorrel, some strawberry, clover, and dandelion. The stems and leaves are longer because the spaces between the hay are larger, with fewer areas of dense frost. I would assume hay to be the best cover for plants to grow in, although "weeds" come from the hay, and it was harder to keep track of the plants there. I covered "cultivated" spaces with hay. "Cultivated" spaces might have had plugs taken from the food field that had been put two to three inches apart in a plain dirt area, growing to solid sorrel, or clover, just for easier access when I went out front with a pair of shears to harvest! These areas were hayed for convenience and the clover, for instance, was already tightly seeded for the next year.

LAUNDRY DAYS

I welcomed the experiences and accepted the challenges of our early homesteading days—they were times of trial and error. One challenge I had to accept was learning to wash clothes in the wilderness. Before one year was out, I certainly did understand why man invented the washing machine.

Then, after ten years of washing clothes by hand in streams, lakes, tubs, and buckets, I found an antique washing machine (circa 1880) for sale.

It consisted of a frame, two buckets, a plunger and a wringer. Blankets were usually a chore to wash, but were done quickly with the new machine. The spring floods almost carried off my machine, but we rescued it from a foot of mud and silt and brought it back to solid ground. I used bushes to spread the clothes on for drying and did not buy a clothes line for ten years.

Winter buckets of wash water were hauled one by one. A total of five buckets of water was needed to wash, and six were needed to rinse the laundry. Heating the water was not a problem because the stove was kept warm day and night and was always ready to accept pails of water.

Chopping a hole in the ice in the winter was an exercise in frustration—the water instantly froze in the buckets because of forty below temperatures.

After that, defrosting gigantic icicles was the solution, and so much faster than hauling water by the bucket. I was grateful for the unwinterized camp when it came to "harvesting" dozens of icicles. The roofs were full all the time!

BATHING

The rocks were miraculously placed in the rushing river. Large, flat rocks growing in steps from any season's water flow. Close to the bank and easily climbed down too, the bath rocks were a special, natural tub.

I chose to take my bath at odd times, from first thing in the morning to late at night. The hot, noon ones were the most delicious. I always waited on the steps for a moment, listening for anyone's approach. I knew the bird's signal if a lone hunter approached, or a very rare hiker trekked close enough to see my personal moment!

Sometimes the river water was unusually warm. These baths were my best memories—the dragonflies zooming near, the warm sun on a wet day, the rush of the water with its occasional lapping on the bath rock. To dangle your legs and feet in this succulent moving pool was connection to pleasure!

Soap was of many substances. Homemade, even from plant bases was not done too often. Luckily I had occasion to visit the local general store that had luscious bars of homemade soaps with different flavors. I made this purchase a special personal one for many years. Bargain bars of biodegradable soap were the family's, because the river claimed dozens and dozens of bars between the three of us.

I had some sort of vision how the river looked downstream when they all floated, a bit smaller, to the Cedar River Bridge on the way to Indian Lake. "Oh dear, the homesteaders lost a bar of soap again!"

Hair washing was different! I always made my own shampoo. Cow cockle (bladder campion) was the flower of choice—a green, gooey soap became the best shampoo! I will never forget my daughter Kim elaborating on this concoction. Her friend Jill was visiting that summer. The two teenagers had made a cauldron of bladder campion flowers (soap plant) and to make it more glamorous, they added blueberries, of course, for the blue color! No one told them they would turn the soap rancid and alcoholic in a few hours!

You could hear the two girls giggling at their bath from quite a distance. You could also hear them scream bloody loud when they dumped the foul smelling rancid shampoo over their heads at the same time. The "Eeeew!!" flowed from their mouths as they jumped in the river.

On a negative note, the bath sometimes was a nightmare of wash, dry, and dress quickly while the black flies and mosquitoes ate your clean patches of skin. Working with the agility of speed demons, the insects attached by the hordes. Sometimes I returned with splotches of blood from swatted mosquitoes and puffy eyes from the agile black flies. My son would ask, "When are you going to take a bath, Mom?"

CRAWFISH HUNTING

The Cedar River flows quietly and has shallows where crawfish breed and live. Early in August the crawfish hide in the river's crevices and under its rocks. The rocks are being turned ever so slowly by hand, as I reach in and out of the water. A pail is strung on my waist and I am a huntress.

Wading to my knees, slow movement is very necessary near the edges of the currents. Gazing down to the sunny, sandy bottom, I can see the tail sticking out by a large rock. The fantail scuttles, scuttles hard, kicking up clouds of sand as my hand flashes down through the water sideways.

Slicing a silent, curved path behind the fantail, I scoop him up quickly and flip his bony body into the pail. Scuttle, scuttle. Gray bodies, pink, white, bluish-white all scuttle from their lairs, and are picked up from the river bottom the same way. Footing is precarious and thick algae coats the rocks in some areas. I choose

spaces in between and pinch the crawdads, easily. Dragonflies rise from the reeds and the mosquitoes zip about in and around the heat surrounding the hunt. Feeding time has come now.

Fish appear from their lairs and break water on the river's edges. The crawfish disappear completely. I am satisfied with my catch and return to camp with enough bait for the family to use for trout fishing. I am looking forward to the next hunt already.

Thank you, river, for giving up your gifts to me.

PAILS

All throughout the homestead years pails became a daily tool. Uses were extensive. Some daily uses were:

      Gathering drinking water, bath, or wash water,
      Heating water on the stove, doing dishes,
      Carrying slop water,
      Carrying coals to put under frozen car,
      Holding bait, fish, crawfish, worms, greens,
       pods, nuts, berries,
      Washing food,
      Washing hair,
      Carrying sand, dirt, pebbles,
      And hundreds of other uses.

Pails wore through all too often. At first a pin hole leak of water appeared. That pail was cycled to other uses besides liquids. The hole was sometimes sealed again by taking the pail into the Indian Lake gas station to be soldered. Pails were picked from the dump if no obvious hole was detected. At times  the pail was all right, just dented, or sometimes filled with debris and thrown out. Over the years dozens and dozens, little and big, plastic and metal pails were well used. Big five-gallon lard or icing pails were scoured and used. I was always on the lookout for a free, thrown-away pail. A use would become known soon!

SIMPLE TRICKS

Here are some hints from my living in the wilderness:

I take several ends of branches from a needle tree such as spruce, balsam or pine, and overlap them to make a screen for herbal drinks or teas.

I always carry strips of birch bark and waterproof matches with me. Wax-tipped matches can save the day.

I put my fires out by using dirt or wet moss if water is unavailable. I roll the logs over and over, banging off the loose coals. After completely covering them with dirt and moss, I'd stamp the logs.

Choosing a campsite depends on how many animals are in the area. I look all around at signs, prints, clawed trees, and any velvet. If I see several that indicate many homes and much activity, I move on because I feel like I am intruding.

When I camp near a stream, I am careful to camp on the side that gets the least spray of water. You can see this easily in cold weather. The spray ices the rocks, moss, and one side of the stream bank; it is like moss growing on the opposite side of the spray.

I always put things I want

to find again in stumps, in trees or hanging from limbs. If I know that snow is coming soon, split wood is easy to see if it is piled on a stump.

Use low tree crotches to store your food while gathering. When you come back through the woods, the bunches of food look like a natural trail. You can string your bundles together. There is nothing more aggravating than trying to cut bundles of food when your string of food keeps falling off or getting tangled.

Stupidly, I was amazed when I first tapped trees to find that the taps we had placed were higher up the tree when it thawed. When the snow is four feet deep, you have to take this into consideration.

This theory also applies to cutting wood. Cut the stump low even if you have to dig in the snow to clear it.

When digging for food in the winter, follow a tree down to the south side where snow is the least, or below the side of a rock that is away from the snow path.

A wild food hint is to completely cover areas of clover and dandelion with eight to twelve inches of leaves. Hay works well also. This coverage creates a greenhouse effect. After an early thaw, with four to six inches of snow on the ground, I would uncover and eat the delicious treats of fresh-grown, tiny leaves. They grow well under the warmth of old rotted leaves.

I like to draw, and often used the charcoal from my campfire for my drawing tool. But when I was really serious, I poked holes in the top of a tin can lid and cut twigs of cherry or tag alder into lengths to fit the tin. I dropped the whole can into the fire with the top up. The curls of smoke turned darker and darker grey until it was black. Then, I grabbed the tin with tongs and set it aside to cool. Any sticks that were not now charcoal done were dropped back into the fire for five more minutes. This is how to create a homesteading artist's supply of drawing sticks!

MUD SEASON

Mud season is an indescribable time to the Adirondack inhabitants. Sometimes after the winter's blanket of snow has thawed, the wet woods become thirsty enough to rain again. Mud season begins. A fun time for me. I feel like a kid in a mud puddle, but stepping in and out of oozing mud becomes a real physical chore. Sometimes mud season lasts for two months. This time of the year I crave greens. Searching for them in solid mud is an experience. Cedar River camp was down a dirt road, eight and a half miles from town. To drive there and back in mud season was an enormous challenge. The old green truck was my guide up Potato Patch Hill, with its tricky set of curves before the mill yard. My destiny was to learn to drive as though I were a participant in the Le Mans racing experience in France.

The trick was easy. Approach the hills, and slip your mind into automatic. Wing your way into the ruts, climbing over so steadily. Avoid the deeper eight inch ones, and slide in and out of the four or five inch ones. My speed always slowed down far too quickly, and I would puddle out near the top of the second hill. If you went too fast your vehicle would slip into the eight inch ruts and you hoped no one was coming up at fifty.

Next pass, gain speed, go faster and bingo, you could make all three hills. Can't say this experience gave me any particular feeling but pure panic, some satisfaction when I made it, and great faith in other forces besides my own judgment. I feel WELL qualified to drive the Le Mans any time of the year.

It was easier in the winter on ice. The high scraper banks at least catch your bounce when you slide down backwards on a sheet of glass.

No wonder they say the Adirondacks breeds old dented trucks.

THE NIGHT THE SAW MILL
BURNED DOWN

The night the mill burned down had been extra busy for me. It was a sub-zero day, perhaps ten below. Winds were around twenty miles per hour and picked up about dinner time. A storage shed had been my project for the day. I rolled small logs into place, pounded a few pegs, and sheet metaled the top into place with special sheet metal screws found in the dump.

The "yard" around the camp looked clean, and Todd had a hiding place amongst the boxes, pails, tarps, and odds and ends. Ken, finished with a trimmer-saw man's day of work (about twenty thousand pounds of board that day) came home for a wild food dinner. The mill was shut down for the night. About seven o'clock p.m. I couldn't keep my head up, I just had to curl up and sleep for a few minutes. I awoke with Todd's voice shouting and him shaking me. "Mommy, Mommy, the sky is on fire! The sky is on fire!"

Panic ensued. The mill was burning to the ground. Ken flew from the camp and I grabbed Todd and glued myself to the window, calmly planning an escape route to the river and ice floes. I hadn't the faintest idea if the woods were on fire, fuel tank had exploded, or what. Flames licked the sky, and I knew the danger could be extreme. Ken burst in the door shouting, "The fuel tank is going to blow and we have to run for it NOW!"

Todd kept up with Ken easily, but I had much trouble in the foot of snow, uphill. My legs felt like iron after a half mile, but I gave myself orders, "Keep going, keep going." Things got cartoonish when I looked over at the mill. It didn't even look real. Flames forty, fifty feet high, seemingly in slow motion, licked the five hundred gallon fuel tank with caressing waves. "It has to blow," I said, "Keep going." Ken and Todd were in the truck on the main road as I remembered a strip of dirt road to the truck. I have no memory of the last hundred yards, but in a foot of snow, and boots, found myself at the truck side door, Todd shouting, "Come on! Come on!" Ken had started the truck and in a second we were racing down an icy road for help.

The Indian Lake fire fighters came in force, some forty men battled the fire for hours, keeping the fuel tank from going. They had to hook up hoses at the river, one-half mile from the trucks in the mill yard. Icy conditions and a forty mile wind didn't help any. I stuck by the coffee and doughnuts and prayed a lot. Nothing blew up! No one got hurt! Thank you, God, and thank you, Indian Lake Fire Department.

The era of the log mill was over for me, but the experiences are etched in my mind forever. In later years on a farm I had constant memories, from the sights, sawed lumber, chips, and the smell of raw pine, to the sight of log cuts, perlins, and especially the log men who built the structure.

THE SAWDUST HEAP

Our family stayed for four years on the Cedar. The sawdust heap rising from the past location of the mill was a plus for everyone. I can still see Todd skiing off the lower part of this iceberg of sawdust. Zipping over the crests like a pro on a tiny homemade pair of plywood skis. "Again! Again!" he would shriek.

But, watching all three children was more than I could handle, and I made an excuse to go back to camp. Eric would take a plastic sled and careen over the ice crests with a more than deadly speed. Kim would carefully plan her course and it seemed a breathtaking speed over the mountain crests. Spills occurred, sending my heart up in my throat, and I could not take the scene.

The sawdust heap is an accumulation of years and years of board feet, and stands as a monument to a past of logging business. The crests were 6 or 7 stories tall. Climbing to the top on a clear day one could survey the Cedar River, winding towards Indian Lake, and the Hudson, into which it feeds.

To a child, this heap becomes a Himalayan experience. Digging your hands or feet into a sawdust heap one feels tremendous heat, and some days the heap would catch on fire, belch flames, and we all cried, "The sawdust heap is on fire again." In a week or so, the steam and flames would subside and the area was safe to play on again.

Eventually the insides were hollowed out and the heap was declared off-limits to my children. It became a gun club target range and is still a magnificent monument to an era passed.

THE FIREPIT TURKEY

Thanksgiving was here at last. I was thrilled to have all my children here at the camp. Of course, the hunt was on for a wild turkey. The hours produced no turkey or pheasant. A few dollars had been saved in a mason jar, so off to town I drove in the old green pick-up truck to buy a turkey.

A spit was built over the firepit. A skewer and crank were primitively put together. The three children laughed at the setup, but cranking the bird while it dripped goodness became a fun thing. Turns were taken and I kept coals hot underneath, replenishing wood when needed.

Testing the brown bird proved a tedious task. Every 15 to 20 minutes I proved the bird was not ready. Time stretched through lunch, well into the afternoon. Plenty of hours to fix stuffing and prepare a vegetable. Raspberry jelly and biscuits topped the meal.

DISHES

The dishpan sat on the grey slab table stretched between two birch tree stumps, with the woods before it. The water for the dishpan was hauled by hand and the soap we used was biodegradable.

I was able to splash and not worry about getting water on the floor or the walls because I washed the dishes outside on that table. So washing dishes became a fun chore. Only thunderstorms, black flies or blizzards changed the pattern of gathering water and enjoying every moment of washing the dishes.

Cooking the meals outside was as handy as that dishpan on the slab table. The nature around me became the world quickly: chipmunks running under my legs to catch drops of rinse water on a hot August day; Monarch butterflies by the dozens, stretching and re-stretching their orange wings, dipping their coiled tongues in and out of the wet puddles left in the dirt. Some birds had the courage to run under the table and, as with all outdoor experiences, the insects become the challenge to stay in tune with in a positive way.

As I started the fire to heat the rinse water, smudging became the rule of thumb, but usually after a meal was completed. Putting the large cauldrons on with the dish water became a pleasant routine instead of a drudgery.

The experience was an exciting, relaxing part of the day, usually after dinner, but on occasion, I rose with the birds and "cleaned" house before a food gathering day.

BOBCAT, AGAIN!

Experience number three with bobcat came in 1975. This time was not quite as benign as the first two times. Our family was raising rabbits at the time and the nests under the shanty were filled to capacity. It was winter and because there were snow drifts all around, I had no idea how many families were under there. They were comfortable in winter's grip.

The scream of the baby rabbit jolted my mind to consciousness around 3:00 a.m. The snow lay in four foot drifts and pockets. I did not register either time nor snow, NOR the fact that I was barefoot and wearing baby-doll PJ's. Flying from the quilts, I never said a word to my husband. I curled my fingers around the broom handle and bolted from the camp.

I tracked the sound of the squeaking bunny and have no memory of the first few yards in the snow. I found myself wading in drifts with a broom extended murderously overhead. I focused on the blur of fur, galloping ahead of me. The cat exploded up and down in the drifts holding a baby rabbit in his teeth. Another lunge, another screech from the bunny, and the cat turned and faced me squarely.

Wham! I came down with the broom. The bunny flew from his teeth, and the cat recoiled from the blow, whirled and streaked out of sight in a scalloping fashion in and out of the drifts. I gently picked up the moving bunny and climbed up the log step to the camp, after following my trail back.

I was aware of being frozen and grabbed a towel to tend to my legs. I toweled the bunny off gently, noting two holes in his back along with a little blood. He might be all right, I thought, as I crawled back into bed. I deserved the criticism about frostbite and as time would have it, Red became our favorite bunny. Thank you, again, God.

COY DOGS

The Adirondack inhabitants call them coyotes. The coy dog is a yellow, mangy dog about two feet high and extremely wily. They breed and run in packs of about twenty to forty dogs. They work as a team, with an eerie, high-pitched cry that is part hoot and part laugh. They are a menace to the area and have killed dozens of house pets. They love to run deer, hamstringing their victims and never touching the meat for food. The most experienced hunter will never see one, and they are extremely difficult to trap. Never having harmed a person, the coy dog has become the predator of deer in the Northeast.

My first experience with coy dogs was one of sheer terror. I thought the house was surrounded by wolves. I counted forty or more voices in the circle around the old frame house on Abanakee Road. Then dead silence. Needless to say, I bolted the door. I learned that the pack will play this exploratory game with newcomers.

A similarly frightening confrontation occurred one time in the middle of the forest. I was gathering dead poles for stacking on the sides of a teepee big enough to sleep six. I was surrounded, and what I heard was deafening! Chirping, howling, chattering, laughing and hooting. At first I thought aliens were finally here! I soon realized it was coy dogs that were all around me. While running deer, the wild dog pack had come to a screeching halt at my campfire and activities. I lost sight of the deer beyond my eye perimeter, but I saw the dogs quickly and silently surround me.

There they were, slinking from tree to tree on all sides of my vision. Like wolves, silently now, and looming here and there, slowly slinking and looking— twenty or thirty of them. I stoked the fire higher and grabbed my double-bit axe. I was secure and almost

enjoyed their wild games for five long minutes. At last they silently melted into the forest.

The next time I dealt with coy dogs was in the deep woods near our Cedar River home while I was gathering food. A pack ran a deer toward me, so I decided to climb a tree and wait. I heard the deer come crashing out of the woods on my right; she had been hamstrung and was bleeding heavily. Her body thrashed about helplessly. I whooped and yelled, but this didn't seem to affect the scene at all. The dogs had chased the doe for about three miles and she was dying already. I could not summon help so I paid my respects.

A few nights later I heard their cries again. It was 3:00 a.m. I flew down to the trail. I was soundless, and when I got to the bridge I saw them. Black shadows of all sizes, the pack was swarming at the rear of a deer that was struggling into the river. I yelled and hollered, and they ran back into the woods while the deer swam safely away. They stopped using that particular trail and I never saw the pack again, but continued to hear their distant cries—the Adirondack call of the wild.

THE BRIDGE

The 70's fairly exploded with new and exciting experiences. The cabin was nestled deep in dense woods. The Cedar River roared by close to the cabin. Over the river spanned an old log bridge built many long years ago. The creaks and groans were heard many times from the hot boards warmed in the sun.

Cedar River became a center for our family. Washing foods and ourselves, fishing, swimming, crawfish hunting, and watching deer, coy dogs, raccoons, bobcats were but a few activities at the old bridge.

Often I looked at the old deep cracks, marveling at the millions of pebbles trapped here. I was always scanning the large diameter of the grey logs as they swayed and groaned on the river tides. I loved to crouch below safely awaiting a particularly violent thunderstorm. Unwritten rules told me exactly which lightening crash to make a fast barefoot run up the dirt path to camp. The screen door slammed shut with a bang-swat.

The day ice tore the log bridge out was almost like a cartoon to my eyes. I walked off the bridge and trudged in snow about twenty to thirty feet. Ice jams of Alaska-like proportions were against the bridge.

I heard a very loud boom, crack, and groans as the ice floe pushed the logs up and the entire log bridge exploded like Tinker Toys right in front of my eyes. My landlords had built this bridge and I was heartsick for my friends, as well as for my family. An era had passed.

P.S. A real rope trestle bridge was built in its place, tying the other side of the river to us again.

SIX WEEKS IN A TENT

After several years in our saw mill cabin the future demanded a move to a larger trailer. In order to clear that North River land by by hand, one must live in a tent on the property.

Unexpectedly, my children came up for a two-month visit during the muddiest rainy season we had experienced in the Adirondacks. Imagine three teens in two handmade tents. Using tarp, sticks and logs, the challenge was almost insurmountable in the rain and mud. Much giggling, yelling, and arguing ensued, but by night all the teens settled in for a damp night's sleep.

The next day drying racks were built, dry wood stored, tents patched and re-hung, campfires built, boots dried, drinking water drawn, and food gathered for five people. Many sing-songs, games, stories ensued and after three weeks a trip to Indian Lake laundermat was made. "Whew! Clean, dry clothes!" With the sun peeping through, the next three weeks were spent clearing our land, and with heeps of friends we brought a new home into the rustic life. This family weathered

the storm with ease . . . Ha! The woods echoed laughter and giggles in my mind, lasting me the rest of the summer and memories of tents and mud forever.

WALKING DOWN A STEEP, ICY HILL TO OUR NEW HOME

Adirondack winters were special on North River Hill. It could sleet, rain, hail, snow and ice all in one day, and at one time! If the storm didn't produce a ferocious wind, you might get what I called an "ice fog." An ice fog mists the surfaces of everything and freezes it to a thick glaze of ice.

No matter how you look at it, walking isn't easy in the woods on a snowy, icy surface, and going down a steep hill is very tricky. Our new home was nestled just three hundred feet below one of these hills. Going down the hill at the end of the day became a dreaded exercise. I would fall through a couple of feet of snow and catch myself quickly with one hand, groceries in the other arm. My forefinger always seemed to connect, tip first; I broke four fingers on this hill. Each trip down began with the promise not to fracture another bone.

At night, with faint moonlight to guide my way, I picked my way carefully down this path using footholds, saplings and large rocks. I used every bit of energy to get from the bottom of the hill to the door of the house. Water puddled at the bottom of the hill and froze solid.

One night I succumbed to the drudgery of picking my way downhill, and tore the lid off a pizza box I was carrying. I set the groceries between my legs and sat down on the cardboard sled. I pushed off and prayed for the best. Every bit of air expelled from my body in a scream and I came to a miraculous halt at my son's feet. He ran inside the house, laughing hysterically, making the whole maneuver worthwhile!! That was the first and last time I used a pizza box, and I returned to picking my way down the hill.

An addition to our trailer home.

108

NORTH RIVER HILL

I do not know the exact footage of this hill, but for years I heard three miles long. I believe it! This hill provided many hair-raising memories leading to a stronger and stronger belief in God's Supreme Power.

Let's begin with a three-mile long sheet of glass, all down hill. I had started down in my Volkswagon when I realized the dry pavement had a gloss and I began to slide sideways down, down the sheet of glass. Blank spaces in my memories were from complete fear. Carefully I attempted to keep on the right but there was no control of the car. I tried to tap the brakes, each time causing a sideways movement to the right or left from the rear of the car.

There were slightly flatter areas as I went down, and one of them was my hope of getting the car moving right. At the third such area I turned onto the shoulder and finally slammed to a halt. Many hours passed before the gravel and salt trucks rescued me. I continued on down to find dozens of other cars on the shoulders of both sides. Fortunately not one seemed damaged.

The second hair-raising drive began from the bottom of the hill. A country store was located on the bottom road leading to the hill. We all traded there for small items on a weekly basis. One conversation with the owner got around to how cold it was getting that day. A rain had washed us clean and wet several hours ago. By the time I had traveled up the hill about a mile, elevation and cold became alarming, causing sheets of black ice. I decided to go back down the hill rather than try to continue up. Pulling to the rail, the pebbly, sandy shoulder helped me feel safe to stop. Could I make a U-turn quickly enough? But, here it comes—a giant, fully loaded log truck!

I headed back down towards the black ice areas, found a place to stop, jumped out of my car, leaped up the bank, and prayed. My visions imagined the thousand-ton truck spinning side to side, taking my car with it in its hellish, out-of-control spin. But as I scrambled up the bank, the truck passed just like normal, no spin or out-of-control movements, and to this day I am sure the immense weight of that vehicle kept it in control. I jumped in my vehicle, made a U-turn carefully, and quickly headed to safe turf until the salt and gravel trucks came. (I rode on the shoulder all the way down, just in case!)

THE OLD PIANO

I was heartsick without a piano. Since I was six years old, piano music was my mood expressions. During my high school years there were jazz recitals, plays and making LP records for Mom's and Dad's birthdays and anniversaries. These records became treasures for me to hear, as well as for my mother and father.

My life in the woods was entirely different now. When I went into the firehall in town, the chance to play an old upright drew me into the past. I played several times during the first few homesteading years!

Later on I became satisfied with playing the piano one or twice a year. I remember on one occasion, perhaps a wedding or graduation at the firehouse, I wandered over to the old upright and sat down. In seconds, the honky-tonk tunes were rolling on the keys again. Wow! I really did enjoy myself for twenty minutes. I didn't forget after all.

A few weeks went by and winter was closing in fast. A four-wheel truck came down the hill towards our camp and four firemen climbed out. In the back of the pickup was the very same piano. In minutes, the rinky-tink old piano was in our trailer. Winched in by a "come-a-long", the men accomplished the task easily.

"Keep the tunes going," one man said. Before I had a chance to thank all four men, the truck pulled out and returned to the firehall.

A glorious three to four weeks playing all I could remember is a treasured memory for Todd and me. I began to notice notes disappearing, one at a time. After awhile, I had to stop playing as most of the notes were gone.

Soon the old piano was winched out onto our old pickup, same way it came in! Of course I had to get to the dump to help winch the relic out. When it landed, the back split off and out rolled mounds and mounds of round DOG FOOD balls, where the mice had stored their winter meals. I shed tears as the piano music left for many years.

THE NIGHT HOWARD CAME

Jenny, our donkey, arrived with a "hay belly". The farm owners in Warrensburg said she was fat. Overfed. Even a well respected ranger, familiar with horses, came down one day to say Jenny had a "hay belly". None of us gave her chubbiness another thought.

She would not haul a thing, no matter how much coaxing. Even the rod and carrot over her nose never worked. Nor did grain. And since we wanted her to graze on the other side of a ten-foot stream, no amount of hours trying to get her to cross it were effective.

Jenny with her hay belly.

Finally I gave in and Ken brought the persuader—a fifty-foot long, inch-thick rope. Tied safely around Jenny, the rope extended across the stream and, forcefully, Jenny was pulled into the stream, running across quickly. Of course, once she got to the other side, she grazed eagerly. When done, Jenny ran the same way back across. Once more, across easier, and after that, just the rope's appearance was enough for Jenny to whirl and race across herself. She demolished the acre of grass on the other side in less than three weeks.

At night, Jenny loved to go up to the "top" of the property, sleeping in a grove of softwoods. Every night, when called, Jenny would come home to her stable stall, usually before the pitch black of night. This night she was nowhere in sight.

Our area did have bears. I went up to the silhouetted softwood grove of trees, calling her name as I went. A few feet near the trees, I called again, "Jenny, Jenny, where are you?" The donkey shuffled out, slowly. Moving so slowly that I thought she was injured. Ha! Bear! I became on even higher alert.

Out of the brush, Howard staggered. At first I thought he was a young bear cub. Immediately he moved close to his mother. Wow! I remember an overwhelming joy! I shouted, "A miracle, a miracle!" I shouted all the way home as Jenny and Howard followed me to the stable.

Work was not Jenny's strong point, but in motherhood, she shone.

Howard

OUT OF THE WOODS

Eventually Todd and I came out of the wilderness. I pursued various jobs, including nursing, but for that I was told I was overqualified. In an effort to figure out who I was, really, and what I should be doing, I found my prayers being answered each time I encountered in my backyard any of the wild foods that had sustrained us during those wilderness years. I realized that I had acquired a wealth of information that few in this current, hectic, frantic world ever contemplated at all.

I had to learn quite a lot about the business end of teaching. My hard-won knowledge went to the many hundreds of people who sincerely wanted to learn the information I had to impart. In the process, I created a number of successful wild food walks, I wrote books, created a survival card deck, and continued my art work.

And along the way, the Wild Food Company was born. It has been over 20 years now, and I give many thanks to lots of people. I can now offer all of my current publications on my website (created and maintained by my webmaster son Eric), www.OfTheField.com. I hope that the information is useful to you.

Breinigsville, PA USA
07 September 2010
244876BV00001B/52/P